The Story of a

Hutchins Hapgood

Alpha Editions

This edition published in 2024

ISBN : 9789362924124

Design and Setting By
Alpha Editions
www.alphaedis.com
Email - info@alphaedis.com

As per information held with us this book is in Public Domain.
This book is a reproduction of an important historical work. Alpha Editions uses the best technology to reproduce historical work in the same manner it was first published to preserve its original nature. Any marks or number seen are left intentionally to preserve its true form.

Contents

Chapter One .... - 1 -

Chapter II .... - 6 -

Chapter III .... - 11 -

Chapter IV .... - 16 -

Chapter V .... - 21 -

Chapter VI .... - 27 -

Chapter VII .... - 33 -

Chapter VIII .... - 40 -

Chapter IX .... - 46 -

Chapter X .... - 53 -

Chapter XI .... - 57 -

Chapter XII .... - 60 -

CHAPTER ONE

I was thirty years old when I saw her for the first time. We did not speak, we were not introduced, but I knew that I must meet her; I knew that love which had hitherto been gnawing in my imagination and my senses, had found an object. I fell in love at first sight. She did not see me—and I sometimes think she has never seen me since, although we are married and have lived together for fifteen years.

Life had prepared me to love. I was born sensitive and passionate, and had acquired more emotion than I was endowed with. I had acquired it partly through ill-health and ignorance as a lad, and partly through an intense sex-imagination to which I habitually and gladly yielded. My boyhood was filled with brooding, warm dreams, and partial experiences, always unsatisfied, and leaving a nature more and more stirred, more and more demanding the great adventure.

Then, in youth and early manhood,—as a student, a traveler,—experiences came rich enough in number. The mysterious beauty and terrible attraction that woman has for the adolescent was not even relatively satisfied by my many adventures. Each left me more unsatisfied than before. My hunger for profound relationship grew so strong that all my ideas of beauty, in art, in life and in nature, seemed to be a mere comment, a partial explanation, of that which was a flame in my soul.

This explanation, this comment derived from art, while the ultimate result was greater inflammation, so to speak, yet often temporarily soothed. This was especially true of philosophy and reflective poetry. I had no interest in metaphysics as such, but when, in the university, the magnificent generalizations of philosophy first came to me, I thought for a time that I had found rest.

Dear Wordsworth! How he cooled my fevered senses and soothed my heart and mind; how he pleasingly introduced into every strong sensation an hygienic element of thought which made the whole into warm reflection rather than disturbing impulse! And dear Philosophy! Who, when taught to see things from the viewpoint of eternity, could be intensely unhappy about his own small Self and its imperfections? In Plato, in Spinoza, in Hegel, Fichte, Nietzsche, Schopenhauer, I felt the individual temperament struggling to free itself, as I had been struggling to free myself, from too great an interest in Self through the contemplation of what seemed to be the eternal and unvarying truth.

But then, with returning strength, there came metaphysical skepticism. These great structures of philosophy seemed to me to be houses of cards, toys for imaginative children. And at the same time there burst upon me, with renewed intensity, the world of sensuous art, the direct, disturbing force of Nature, the mysterious appeal of Woman. Philosophy had prepared me for a greater absorption in life than would otherwise have been possible. It helped to make me incapable of what men call practical life, and made me attach values only to significant things.

And it lent to my most trivial relations with women the spiritual quality of meaning. Even in the midst of transient sensuality, the eternal flow of Nature, and the inherent significance of all sex life, no matter how impersonal and unindividualized, gave a constant and inevitable spirituality. It was a torturing, promising spirituality. It beckoned to something beyond, dropped strangely disturbing hints of what might be. In the midst of kaleidoscopic women, the Unknown Woman was suggested, foreshadowed. These sensual-poetic experiences were purifiers of the amorous temperament, rendering it at once more passionate, more spiritual and more classic, less mixed with prejudice, with the indecency of ignorance, with unclear as well as unclean theological taboos. I went through every phase of so-called coarse sexual experience, and thereby strengthened and purified my spiritual demand for the Great Adventure. If I had not known women, I should never have known woman; nor could I have loved Her so essentially, so absolutely as I have.

With this past behind me—a past full of the pleasures of thought and sense, of the pain of self-doubt, of strenuous struggle for self-realization, for self-understanding—I met Her. In spite of my thirty years, I was as youthful as a faun endowed with a mind and who had recently partly escaped from a theological conception of life. From the Present of Paganism I looked back to the sensual struggles of escape from the secondary results of a defeated theology.

And she! How different her nature and her past from mine! She had never struggled with herself. She did not need to, for herself did not disturb her. Imperturbable, she struggled only with her work, with what she was trying to form. She was an artist, and singularly unconscious of herself. Keen to external beauty, she was not interested in the subjective nature of her Soul, or its needs, or how it worked. In fact, her soul seemed to have no needs. I often told her she had no soul, but I was wrong, as we shall see.

Along one of the corridors of the world she passed me for a moment, and I knew that I must love her. She was a thing of beauty! It was not merely her lovely skin and hair: she was one of those rich, dark blondes who seem to have absorbed the light and warmth of the sun and to have given it a definite form which introduced the spiritual quality of the brunette—blond in color, brunette in quality. There was nothing bleached about her, nothing faint, nothing iridescent. Her color and quality were that of saturation. It was as if in her skin and hair warmth and color lay suspended, as it lies suspended in dropping summer rain.

But I know it was not her skin and hair that I loved. What I loved I feel now, though I did not analyze it then, was the integrity of her physical and nervous nature. She was no self-conscious neurasthenic, as I was! She was cool, unconscious, poised—cold, the ignorant would call her. And the Silence which breathed from her when I first saw her has been hers ever since. Never, even in agony, has she been noisy. Her deep quiet comes as a disturbing thing, to most people, and it has been often the cause of quarreling between us—for I, nervous, with a volcanic past, frequently challenged this quiet soul, challenged it morally and socially, succeeded, to my immense satisfaction, in disturbing it once or twice, but being more often disturbed and irritated myself!

I maneuvered a meeting, and many, many followed, and have been following for fifteen years. Our first few meetings showed me that she had no past! All that she could or can remember is that she had worked—worked calmly and quietly, without excitement. Her life as a child was as calm as that of a plant. I have a whole world of violent emotions remembered, stretching along from my third or fourth year. She has no remembered childhood. She grew too beautifully, too gradually, too quietly, to have occur those cataclysmic things which one remembers. And she still grows!

I suppose what drew us together was Wonder. I marveled at her strange and beautiful integrity, the wholeness and calmness of her being. My vivid nature, my tremulous needs, my spiritual restlessness, interested her. I loved her, and for me she felt a deep amusement. The strangeness I felt in her seemed beautiful; the strangeness she felt in me seemed interesting and amusing. And for years the only word of approval I ever heard from her was the word "amusing." I can imagine Mona Lisa saying the same word, in exactly the same spirit, meaning intellectually entertaining.

"A thousand years old am I," she would say. And I seemed so young to her; amusingly young. I suppose all lovers are young, no matter how many years they have. And yet it was I who had definite experience, as the world commonly understands that word. And she had had none. And yet she was old and I was young. She was not naïve, she was not fresh. She was like the Sphinx, wonderful, old, with a beauty that to me at times was terrible. And I charmed her because I was so pleasingly social, so civilized, and had so many ideas derived from life, ideas which pleased her mind and stirred her sense of poetry and humor. I loved her for the essence of her being, and she liked me warmly for what I was able to say and feel.

Especially for what I was able to say! How she would listen! I know that if what I have said to her could be recorded, it would pass as literature. I am proud only of that one thing: that to her I talked well—really well—for years. I told her all—all of my life, and I think it must have seemed to her like the life of some inhabitant of Mars. Surely, there was in our relationship a deep unfamiliarity—I was strange to her and she was infinitely strange to me. But I loved her strangeness, and my strangeness only interested her. Being profoundly kind, that interest finally awoke emotion in her—but it was not the love of the real and mysterious spiritual form which is at the basis of every human being. She felt æsthetically my qualities. She did not love Me.

It was this which made me bitter, at times, during many years, and even now comes to me like some essential pain. Quite unjustly so—and yet inevitable. When I saw awaken in her, in later years, some such feeling for other men as I had for her, a feeling not based on what they could say or do or even feel, but on what her imagination told her they deeply *were*, an indescribable rage would take possession of my soul.

Perhaps that rage was merely jealousy, that loathsome feeling based on an incredible sense of possession, but I do not believe that. After my genuine social thought began she might have had all manner of relations with other men, without deep disturbance on my part; I might have been unmoved, had she *seen* me, once and forever! But as I have said, she felt only my qualities, my gifts of the mind, heart, and spirit. She did not have an immediate, temperamental understanding and love for myself! And to have this feeling for some soul is a need of all deep natures. When I saw this need in her—unsatisfied by me—reaching out to others to whom she had no *coherent* relation—only the mysterious, temperamental, almost metaphysical one that we mean when we say "in love"—it was then that the rage came upon me! Was it jealousy? It was strong and terrible, whatever it was, capable of overpowering all the acquired canons of civilization and making of me an incarnate, miserable, bestial Demand!

I imagine that at least a part of this pain is derived, at any rate in my case, from an egotistic sense of something deeply essential that is lacking in oneself. If this deep woman, who admired and warmly liked me in every nameable way, could not feel the temperamental stir, could not feel me as distinguished from the sum of my qualities, what was the matter with me? What did I deeply lack? I had no crude lack. Physically and mentally I was competent. I could meet her desires in every obvious way. Yes! But the Real Self is not obvious. That, to her, was lacking; that most mysterious, and yet to the eye of the amorous imagination, most real thing of all, which needs no expression to manifest itself, *that* she never saw! Perhaps that is lacking in me! This fear may partly account for the pain I felt. What strenuous soul can endure the thought that perhaps he is lacking in a way so deep that it is unanalyzable?

Sometimes I would think that it was my partly-shattered nervous system. How could this woman's nature, with its sweet integrity, love anything but that which had developed in the most beautiful way? I loved her partly because she had grown without harm. I had not grown without injury; and one perhaps cannot love æsthetically, temperamentally, the injured. My very injuries accounted for my eloquence, my intensity of feeling. This naturally would interest, but how could an æsthetic soul love the shattered cause of even fine things? I have never known a keenly expressive person who was nervously sound; and the nervously unsound are not æsthetically beautiful, however productive they may sometimes be of beautiful things. It shows a fine instinct in a woman to love only what in itself is lovely, without materialistic or sentimental regard for what that thing may do, say, or feel.

CHAPTER II

WELL, as I have written, I met her in one of the corridors of the world, and I loved her, and I insisted on her knowing me, or trying to know me. She was working, and I was working, and in the evenings we met in the cafés and restaurants and we talked, or rather I talked. I talked about everything—literature, art, sex, wine, people, life,—especially about life! He who does not know very definitely what the indefinite word "life" means has no knowledge of what the essential social relationship between a man and a woman is. A fine woman cares for nothing else. She is not a specialist. And yet most misguided busy men avoid talking life to their sweethearts and wives. They leave the real themes to the unworthy—to rakes, artists, and philosophers, to bohemians and outcasts, or to the very few respectable and at the same time intellectual men who are living on their incomes. And then they are surprised when their wives or sweethearts begin to see with emotions somebody else! Men are for the most part extremely naïve—especially good, sober, industrious, business American men. They are becoming the Predestined ones of the earth, and that is no proof of the infidelity of their wives and mistresses, for they who sow must reap, and Nature will outlive the ethical remnants of an outworn theology. There are one hundred thousand well-to-do wives in the United States today who are deeply disturbed by life, and their husbands do not know that anything but nerves is happening to them.

She liked my talk from the start. But to her it was not disturbing—not then—as it would have been to a less composed soul. To her it was merely contributive. It was one more cool channel to knowledge. From the start I tried, tried hard, to disturb her. I felt that if I could disturb her she would love me. In a sense I was more naïve than the business man! I might have known that love for my words would not lead to love of me, that through my talk she might love life more, not me; her love of life, heightened, enhanced through me, might lead her to see others, not necessarily me! I might easily act as an impassioned medium to the Road of Life along which she might find beautiful forms fit for love. I helped her, as a matter of fact, to see men, to feel their quality, just as she helped me to see women. It is true that had I not known women, I would not have known her; but it is also true that knowledge of her gave me a deeper understanding and the possibility of a more intimate approach to other women.

At that early time, however, I did not realize that at all. I did not know that I was working for others as well as for myself. In a deep sense there is a sort of impersonality, a lack of egotism, in passion. It drives us on, even against our personal interests, or what we narrowly regard as our personal interests. A mind and heart in love with life is never merely personal. One of the intensest passions is to give oneself to something which overpowers one's personality.

Working! Yes, that is the word! I worked for her as I never worked for money, for art, for fame, for duty. No one can know how I have worked who does not know how I have loved. Nothing exhausts like emotion; especially the higher forms of sex-emotion, mixed with temperament and thought and a sense of value as all-embracing as religion. I imagine that the few great artists and doers are they who are capable of this great sex intensity but who through some kind of happy perversion put this intensity into their art or deeds and so strike out great forms. Only in white heat is a great thing created—a human being, or an art form or a sublime social thought, or an act of transcendent meaning for the race. Had I been carried by as inevitable a passion to make an epic in art, or to live an epic in social struggle as I have been to commune with a human temperament, I might well have been looked upon by my fellow men as one of the great ones of the earth. But few of us who have the necessary intensity are willing, even if we are able, to make this sacrifice—for it is a sacrifice. We are impelled irresistibly to exhaust ourselves on the proper object, as is the moth devoted to the devouring flame. To withhold ourselves from the proper object of passion is the perversity of heroic self-denial.

She married me at last without being more than deeply pleased. My warmth and my impassioned ideas became a necessity to her. Life without me would in some measure have lacked richness. It was after a year of strenuous wooing on my part—a struggle which involved all my mental, moral and emotional resources. Before she knew me she needed nothing. I had taught her to need. This she realized when, in a moment of exhausted despair, I left her and tried desperately to live without her. After a time she wrote and I interpreted her letter as a recall. I returned on the wing of desire, and there was a subtle difference in her when we met. She was silent, but her large, mysterious-colored eyes glowed with a half-questioning promise. She seemed to be wondering whether she was destined, after all, to live with me.

We were never engaged to be married. She never passionately committed herself. We grew into marriage. There came a time when she liked to have me hold her in my arms, to kiss her long hours. It was her education, sentimental, sensuous. It enhanced her nature, and it made her nature demand. But it was tantalizingly impersonal. She liked equally well to sit by the seashore and watch the waves and the line of the sky. I have been driven from her arms, where I felt like a happy stranger, by a sudden anguish which in extreme reaction would carry me to the arms of some less-balanced stranger, whose nervous intensity would reëstablish me momentarily into relative feelinglessness.

I remember, on one occasion, when I was in this mood, how I allowed a girl to woo me. She was led to do so by my despair which, keeping me spiritually away from her, provoked her ambition. She passionately desired to overcome what had overcome me. I understood her and was unhappy and brutal enough to allow her to try the impossible. She—the only She—not this poor momentary girl—was never consciously brutal to me, as I was to the other. And yet I constantly reproached her.

I said she had no soul. I said it repeatedly in all manner of ways. I said it when she was warmly hidden in my arms. I said it as we drank wine together across the table of the genial table-d'hôte. I said it between the acts of the theater. I said it in the street-cars and in the open country stretches where we walked. Did she marry me partly because of a kindly desire to prove to me that I was wrong? I did all I could to disturb, to wound, to arouse, to make her calm soul discontented and unhappy; as well as to interest her vividly and constantly. I think the truth is that she married me because she had to. Like Nature I was always there and would not be denied. Water runs down hill without any great desire to get to the bottom.

These things I said to her, of course, as I said all things to her. She would smile one of those quiet smiles that go all through her being, that are as spiritual as they are physical, that are neither and both. Sometimes in her hinting way, she would quietly suggest that if she should try to express herself to me I would run away. She would amusedly call attention to the vanity and egotism in me that demanded above everything else a sympathetic listener. It is beautifully true that she holds all subjects in solution, that she broods over a theme and does not try violently to assert her personality. With her always is going on a process of incubation. With complete pregnancy of thought-feeling and feeling-thought, she waits, waits, knowing that things grow only in quiet. The gods approve the depth and not the tumult of the soul, wrote Wordsworth, the deeply medicinal poet. It is probable that the finest women are like this. Holding all things together, brooding over life, the tumult of the soul is hateful to their natures,—the tumult which sometimes has even a lovely place in the make-up of a man who must have violent relations with an imperfect world. And I do not think that it is only my vanity and egotism which makes me feel so—my intense and morbid desire for temperamental sympathy. That exists, it is true, but in this brooding nature there is something impersonally beautiful, unexplained by my egotistic needs. The seed as it bursts quietly in spring-warmed earth is beautiful, not because it does not interrupt us in our feverish futilities, but because in itself it is adequately and richly significant of the whole urge of life.

It is evident that I need to defend myself against her charge, that if she had been expressive, I would have become cold. The philosophy which I have displayed may not be sufficient. What is significant, however, and I think conclusive, is the fact that on the rare occasions when she became expressive to me and to others, I did not tend to withdraw from her; on the contrary, I felt nearer to her, nearer in a new way, nearer through perceiving in her a slight touch of the weakness I knew so well in myself.

Marriage had in me the typical and rightly typical result. It cured me, for the time being, not of love, far from it, but of the diseases of love. For a long time I had neglected the world for her. I could not work, except perfunctorily. My best friends, whom I used to spend long hours with, I found pale and uninteresting. Books were tedious, had nothing to do with the truth of life. Relatives were well-meaning, but boresome. Often I reflected how normal and right the hero of d'Annunzio's "Il Trionfo della Morte" was, when, separated even for a week from his mistress, most poignant boredom would descend like an active pall upon his soul! Formerly I had thought him diseased, neurasthenic. But now he seemed gloriously normal; he had the rightness of the Superman about him. It was only the other day I received a letter from a lover whose sentiment came to me as something deeply familiar. "This experience," he wrote, "has made me even more impatient than ever of stupids, bores and sillys. It has burned the inessential out of me with regard to human commerce."

"Burned the inessential out of me!" Yes, it does that. And it makes us pathetically dependent on the essential. If we have not that, we have nothing, when we are in love and without the possession of the desired one.

But with possession, blessed state! comes again into our ken the world with its varied interests, and all more wonderful than before! When I felt secure in the possession of my beloved everything else acquired fresh beauty in my eyes, and I could be without her and yet happy and deeply interested in what I was doing and experiencing. My friends became my friends again, my work my work, and it all had a glow of added meaning. I was wiser, and happily wiser than before, and understood more of the nature of the beautiful. The delicious creature had made the universe more delicious to me than ever.

And the honeymoon! This wonderful time that makes happy and normal at once—that gives color and joy and sensuous pleasure and at the same time frees one from the too great intensity of an unsatisfied desire! The wonderful, ornate honeymoon when the full beauty of your mistress is revealed to you, but when this beauty has the cooling and pleasing and caressing quality of Nature and no longer corrodes and harasses and waylays and deeply troubles! The sleepless, wonderful nights, the wonderful languid days following, the infinite noon embraces, the infinite talks and hopes and plans; and the sensuous April quarrels, the life-giving rain of them, the hot and liquid reconciliations! The melting joy of it! The glorious health of it; the senses gloriously stirred and gloriously satisfied!

CHAPTER III

LOOKING back on that honeymoon now, after a lapse of fifteen years, it seems so simple, so naïve and so lyrical! It was before the beginning of what seemed to me later the complexities of life, the intricacies of human relations, those many-hued and contradictory threads which render dangerous the love relation and threaten its duration, but at the same time prevent its atrophy. And in spite of the danger there is something that urges on every strenuous lover to dig deeper down into the wonderful being he is living with. It is a sound instinct which tells us that unless there is development there is death. We see in all Nature the law that to keep the life we must build up the body, whether it be the individual body or the body of a relationship.

And yet we, poet-lovers, struggle against the passing of the simple into the complex! The lover passionately wills the continuing of the same, but deeper than his will is his unconscious instinct which is preparing the unknown addition, the fascinating new danger. I remember, as if it were yesterday, her despair when she first knew she was to have a child. It was not so much because she felt the impending change in our relation—for, as I have written, I was not then and am not now sure that she ever fully accepted that relation—as it was the intrusion into her nature and life of something unknown and seemingly foreign. She rebelled consciously against the breaking up of her integrity, of that breathing wholeness of her being which made life, work and love seem mere aspects of the same simple thing.

This child was thrust upon her as my love had been thrust upon her. It was something she did not consciously welcome. And yet deeper than her consciousness—and of this she was well aware at a later time—was the need of that disturbing change. I know she wanted the child with a want deeper than her will, and this conviction has often made me feel that she wanted my love more than she knew. My love and the children that resulted were the tools that Nature used whereby she might continue to live, through change and development.

What obscure joy this pregnancy was to me! One early morning I awoke and saw her lying asleep by my side, and on her belly were traced the first lines of the new Life. As she lay there, with this plastic sign of the coming child incarnate on her lovely body, I was filled with a wild exultation, and I clasped her passionately in my arms.

How can I account for the intense joy I felt in what was to her at the time a conscious burden? I did not reason about it. I could not have explained it satisfactorily to myself. Why should I rejoice in the discomfiture of the creature I loved? It was perhaps the unconscious knowledge, the instinct for life which made me ecstatic—I knew without thought that greater life had been meted out to her, to me, to all. I was glad that she was to be destroyed, so that she might rise again from the ashes of her old unconscious conservatism. "Each man kills the thing he loves," wrote the poet, but he also renders possible for the beloved another and a larger life. Thus destruction and rebirth go hand in hand, and so I could not find it in my heart to regret, as she lay weeping in my arms.

Life is spiritual. The simple things are the great mysteries. What must happen is the only beautiful. The accidental is never lovely. Her first pregnancy was to me a source of never-ending wonder and delight. The richness, the color, the quiet of it! The sensitive calmness that pervaded her whole being! The lovely adjustment of what she had been to what she was about to be. What poise at each step, what breathing, expanding life! How she seemed in deep unconsciousness to brood like a spirit over her wonderful body—the body that was as much a part of her as her spirit. It was her spirit, as her spirit was her body,—both were different aspects of the same.

It was a time of weeping sensibility. A slight intrusion of anything not a part of her enlarging nature brought quick tears and seemed to cast a shadow over the pervading sunlight of her condition. I remember, as we sat one day under a pine tree, I threw at her in play a light little cone which barely touched her life-breathing skin. But it was enough to disturb the powers that were intent on their wonderful purpose. And the tears that followed were a silent and unconscious rebuke. I who should have guarded her against any unfriendly intrusion was guilty of a deep offense. She did not say so, perhaps did not think so, but her whole being knew so. The sin was greater because not intended. I and the rest of external Nature were in duty bound to be more sensitive. And, of course, she was profoundly right. The great sins are unconscious and inevitable, due to the coarseness of the Universe.

The throwing of the cone was symbolic of much of my relation to the woman I loved. In moments of intensity I felt the spiritual meaning of all Life, and at such times I could understand, at least, how to act with sensibility towards her. But much of the time I was carelessly throwing figurative cones, projecting acts and thoughts which were intruders, which did not make a sweet part of the complex, the total content of her nature, but were hostile to it. Perhaps it was this which made our relation so often a troubled one, and which has left in me a deep, lingering sense of doubt of her love for me. She has never accepted my Form, my essential Self, as beautiful. Flashes in my acts, thoughts and feelings have some approach to what is friendly to her spirit, but the whole thing is not sensitized and intensified enough to form the blue flame of perfection which her soul desires.

And my coarse conceptions and brutal acts were of far greater dimensions than those of the cone. I demanded a continuity of emotion and a constantly repeated experience. For me there must needs be something significantly active; in me always was a restless reaching out, a striving to connect myself with something foreign; in a vain, unconscious hope of finding the rich peace that did not exist in my own soul, I went out to every passing thing, seeking an unattainable equilibrium. Only restlessly man realizes himself, wrote Goethe. Only by connection with outside things does the male come to the consciousness of himself, if he be a pure male, which is an ugly misfortune. And the only way he rids himself of this undesirable purity is by the disillusion bound up in his nameless, continuous superficial acts. He ever approaches but never attains the brooding dignity and sensitive peace of the pregnant woman.

The soul of every beautiful thing is quiet. Much of the time she was so quiet and so unresponsive that there was no place for me in her presence. Often I went away from her, irritated by her very perfection; by her self-sufficiency and calm; went away from what I loved and what I prized, to occupy myself with transient things, experiences and strangers—with work, with women, and with boon companions!

These were the cones of more serious character that I threw into the face of this womanly woman! And it is what many a man has done before and since. In him it is the love of life and of play. In play, he throws his cones, as the child gleefully tears from the butterfly its gorgeous wings. In cruel play he seeks and seeks, seeking self-realization wherever he can find it; going through his Pilgrim's Progress, hoping for the Impossible, finding the Illusion. And in this play he is able to continue, to appear to go further, through the unconscious help of the woman he loves! To live intimately with a woman is to learn an instinctive subtlety of approach to all of life, to work, to the understanding of art and of the problems of society, to the more complete friendship with men and with other women.

Yes, with other women! This is not the truth as written down in the sentimental storybooks of life. It is not what we teach our young men, nor, for some obscure reason, is it what we desire to believe. It is contrary to the fictions of Romance. If it has beauty, it is the beauty of a grimmer Realism. It possesses the quality of deep irony, that she should help her lover to Others! And that thereby Others should receive more! But the real romance lies in the return to the Beloved. Her errant Lover is a Retriever who brings rich gifts from the world to lay at the feet of his Mistress.

As I went in and out of the unformed places of the world, in the obscurities and half-lights of the cities of men and women, I gathered up stray flashes and suggestions and carried them piously home to her, as the child on the beach rushes to his mother with his latest find, some delicately traced shell perhaps, for her to admire. If I went away from her, irritated by her inexpressive calm, by the far-away brooding of her soul, and feverishly sought a café-companion, whose abrupt and fragmentary experiences combined into form through my eager sympathy, a part of the pleasure and the impulse that drove me to it was to bring it back to her.

To bring it back to her, to please, interest and disturb her! To exhibit myself, my mental and imaginative resources, to arouse her admiration, to stimulate her senses, to excite her amorousness, to awaken and challenge her perfection! To contribute to her pregnancy, not only of the body, but of the soul and mind, gave me a deep excitement and a satisfaction that passes understanding.

And her brooding soul, the soul of the artist and the woman, working on forms both physical and spiritual, took what came to her, both pain and pleasure, and wove it insensibly into the harmony of her being. At a later time, it was difficult, perhaps impossible, for her to welcome all I tried to force upon her, but during the first years of our married life, she took it all very much as she breathed, naturally, tolerantly, with quiet understanding, never failing to remain herself, but making room for the foreign things that came to her through me.

I wonder if it is not true that the most difficult art in the world is the art of human relations. What we call art is mere child's play in comparison. And a human relationship is never finished, as long as it remains alive. There is a never-ceasing, strenuous re-making, re-creating. It tests everything there is in a man to live artistically with a woman, and it calls out all the art of a woman to insist that her relations with a man shall have essential form.

Patience is as necessary to the art of love as it is to any other art. One may throw off fine sketches impulsively, nervously, but there is a wide difference between the sketch and the finished thing. We find painters and writers who have suggestive ideas but who never put enough enduring intensity into their work to give it essential form. So, too, in the art of love. The rule in love as in the minor arts—these minor arts being poetry, painting, sculpture and music—the rule in love is the sketch. Very few lovers go beyond the sketch. Few have the enduring power, the artistic patience to build the relation into an essential form. It is perhaps for this reason that love is not regarded as an art at all. It is too difficult.

Men and women fall in love with one another. They catch glimpses of that most beautiful thing—that unseen thing—the soul of the opposite sex as incarnate in the body—and under the excitement of that perception, they are in love. But a glimpse is a glimpse, and it passes quickly, in a day, in a year. It passes if it remains thus simple: if it remains merely that vision of beauty. For beauty grown familiar is no longer beauty. It is tedium. It no longer enhances; it no longer awakens, beckons, no longer leads one on.

So most lovers tire quickly. They know love's sad satiety, but if they are real lovers, though not artists in love, they must pass on restlessly from one woman to another, from one man to another, seeking an impossible satisfaction, restlessly, feverishly. They are the sketch-makers. They who have the amorous insight, the love impulse, are usually of this essentially restless kind. They are the minor artists in love, not the great shapers, the patient formers of Life.

But to the artist-lover his Mistress is always unfamiliar. Into her goes all his changing experience. She is remodeled in his eyes from period to period. He sees in the One the incarnation of the Many. Impatient perhaps, superficially, yet deeply he is patient, for he builds his work of art, and is passionately content to build on, if it takes an eternity.

Impatiently I threw at her all the cones I could gather along the Road of Life. I restlessly strove to disturb her, in her ideas, in her feelings; beyond all else I passionately wished to destroy her aloofness, her quiet coolness; even in her pregnancy I would not leave her alone. When I could no longer endure her endurance, when her love of solitude and her almost uncanny quiet, aroused me into a kind of unreasoning indignation, I would, as I have said, rush off and precipitate myself into some sort of restless adventuring; then return and give her the disturbing result of my experiences. But underneath my restlessness and my conventional infidelities, there lay always the deep passionate will for an enduring union, based upon her continuously changing strangeness, the wonderful strangeness, the progressively beautiful strangeness of her nature.

CHAPTER IV

IN our little apartment, in one of the noisiest of New York streets, she waited quietly for the coming of the child. The place had no elevator and one of my clearest memories is the significant difficulty with which she ascended the stairs! She moved with the dignified slowness of unconscious Nature. We used to walk or rather vibrate round the block together for her ominous exercise every evening, so that the child might be well settled down into her womb. Then, after the important task of climbing the stairs, and the less difficult, but still laborious preparation for bed, she would lie back, seeking in vain, complete comfort; full of quiet, full of a wonderful sufficiency, but withal always uncomfortable, with a discomfort as quiet as her pleasures! It was a strange, a beautiful, a laborious time!

Then, in the early evening, with her book and her cigarette, and her quietly insistent burden, what place was there for me? To be with her always at such times would have seemed shameful, even to me. I remember how often I appeared to myself trivial and ridiculous, unkind and superficial, because I wanted to be actively with her, because I wanted her to be actively with me!—to follow my restless talk, to see the pickpocket or the Yiddish poet as I saw them, to sympathize with my quick sympathy for the drunk in the saloon, or the careless girl of my acquaintance!

Even to me in my eagerness I felt the shameful impossibility of it. Big with child, she seemed beautiful in a new way,—and what a way! The inexpressive significance, the wonder of it! So when I went away from her many evenings, leaving her as quiet as her burden would permit, it was with a kind of humiliation. Often have I sallied forth into what was then to me romantic to a degree,—the streets at night, with all their fanciful possibilities of strange meetings, of mental and sensuous suggestions, to meet some man in a café, to follow out the fascinating track to what I hoped would be literature; to what filled me with sketches, sketches of life, mainly unrecorded, but always stimulating and exciting.

I wanted these experiences, but as I left her for them, I felt, as I have said, a kind of shame and humiliation. I seemed to myself to be engaged in trivialities. I could not help comparing myself, restlessly looking into the back-alleys and by-streets of the town and of the world of human nature, with her, lying, voluminous, portentous, waiting, and quietly brooding. I was forced into the street, partly through my nervous curiosity and fever for possible glimpses, partly through my consciousness that she needed more to withdraw herself from me, much of the time, than to be with me. And both these causes did not feed my vanity nor increase my dignity in my own eyes. If I had not been impelled to want these restless contacts, and had been able to be an essential, integral part of her quiet building in a great process, I should have been what my deeper imagination desired. I should have been a part of Beauty itself! But I habitually fell away from my ideal, was continuously thrown off into the amusing futilities of manifold adventures. If I could only have been with child myself! If we could have been with child together! That would have satisfied my deepest instincts, would have made us one. But, limited by inexorable Nature, I was forced to try to impregnate myself in a figurative sense, to wander about the world, led on by the instinctive need of being suggested, of being stimulated into mental and temperamental fruitfulness, into giving birth to ideas!—pale consolations!

If I write sometimes in this narrative about the art of love, do not imagine that I think I know anything about it; nor that in any way I regard myself as successful in this great shaping process. But I have had, and have, a passionate, never-failing desire to do this almost impossible thing. I see my errors and am not sure of the final result. Often I have stood on the brink of failure, and I do so at this moment, filled with a kind of helpless dread, not knowing how to shape the clay of life, to draw the line that is instinctively right, that gives the vital equilibrium of art. I feel at times that this terrific longing of mine is a criminal instinct. Is it not a crime for a man to want to be pregnant? To want to be mutually pregnant? Does it not show a passionate invasiveness, an almost incredible desire for violation of another's personality? Is it not terrible and ugly, rather than beautiful? Perhaps it is both.

And is it not a terrible thing to be dependent on another human being? When we find ourselves going in that direction, should we not strenuously call ourselves to account, and tear the bondage from our breasts? But the greater the need to do so, the more difficult it is; it is really taken from our will and we are the prey of circumstance.

I am now writing many years after the present stage in the story, to which I shall return. I am writing on the brink of the abyss, for I am at a moment when, my love as strong as ever, I perceive with peculiar intensity, the loneliness of our lives, the lack of contact, the complete isolation in which her spirit dwells, and the kind of shrinking that my approach causes in her. Oh, why do I need the Impossible? Why, oh why? She so often tells me, and means it, for she is as clear of guile and as candid as the sunlight, that we could live a happy, pleasant, affectionate life together, if it were not for my obscure, metaphysical needs, my unexplainable passions and the growing restlessness which deprives her of the opportunity for spiritual seclusion. She needs to be emotionally alone, most of the time. Why cannot I endure it?

I can endure now even less than before; for my hope of disturbing her into the need for me that I have for her is growing less, is almost gone. And I am perhaps undergoing what may be called the change of life in a man. There is no physical difference, as far as I can see, but there is a poignant sadness and my vision of the world is changing. It is all as beautiful as before, but now it is the beauty of terror. The universe seemed so friendly, but now it seems to me that all Nature is at war with man, and that we need to gather together and cheer and protect and comfort one another against the external enemy to whom ere long we must succumb. We are fighting a losing fight, and we need sympathy and love and friendship.

It is perhaps that which makes my need of her almost fierce. When the universe fails, the need of a personal relation becomes so intense that all peace is lost. It is said that a woman who is passing through the change of life often undergoes an exaggeration, a stimulation of sexual desire. And perhaps with a man his need for an intense exclusive relation grows painfully greater, as the fire flares up into a brighter flame just before it is extinguished forever and passes into the coldness of old age.

As I write these lines I know the truth does not fully appear. I have an unquenchable desire to tell the truth but it is something that quite surpasses my power of expression. The impression of blackness that these last pages give is not wholly faithful. Blackness is only one color in the compound. I see the whole thing as very beautiful, even separation and death, but I also see the poignant sadness and the quality of terror and tragedy.

As the time of her deliverance from the first born approached, a minor note of quiet gayety modified the harsher noises of life. It was as if the child, which long since had begun to move and stir in the womb, had begun to prevail, and to insist upon a smiling interpretation and a cheerful attitude. The atmosphere of children, in which our relation has existed for an eternity, began to form before the first of our four children was born. As we both together sometimes felt the pulsations of the new life, and she the springing within and the urge and the movement it was the faint suggestion as of a bouncing little cherub playing with his blocks about the room or trying to dive through the window pane! And we would smile together, she one of those long, slow, tender smiles which went through her whole body and soul, and completely satisfied her, and I would smile more quickly, a smile tending to translate itself into a more strenuous expression and a forbidden embrace!

And slowly and richly, like a well-filled argosy, she would sometimes move with me to the café for dinner, and throughout our talk, or more exactly my talk, the unborn would have its effect. It was not like the old days of my pre-nuptial wooing when my words flowed in torrential masses and the atmosphere was filled with the excitement of half ideas and amorous hopes. Into these was introduced a subtle modification. The shadow of the child was cast on the high lights like gray on a water color, bringing in a transfused softening. And my male companions who came alone or with their wives to our little apartment, underwent the same influence, and there was not so much wine and whiskey consumed, and not so much boisterous talk about it and about. The unseen deeper meaning made its demand and insisted upon harmony in the surroundings.

Pregnancy came to seem to me such a normal, inevitable state that when I saw slim girls in the street or young married women who had not yet begun their process of completion, it was with a sort of pity. They seemed so wanting, so forlorn and hoping. Where was the male with his impregnating fierceness? Why should such wanting creatures go thinly about the world?

So natural and beautiful did her condition seem to me that when her pains began, they took me by surprise, though we had been expecting them for many days. It was as if some strange eruption, some volcanic accident had occurred, something quite contrary to the placid course of Nature. It was as exciting and direful as a Revolution! Yet, as I held her hands when the recurrent, ever-increasing pains returned, she in a strange and marvelous way, maintained that calm, that breathing, inexpressible quiet, at which I wonder and shall wonder until my dying day, even though, at times, it has almost driven me mad!

And when, sternly driven by the doctor into the adjoining room, I heard her low, unconscious moans, as the child came ripping from her womb,— deep, suffering sounds which did not seem to come from her but from the world in travail, from the body of Nature itself, sounds not so much human as cosmic, even then there was no turmoil nor violence nor nervousness. It seemed deeply impersonal,—the pain, the sound—to come from the depths of life and death, from a great, a terrible distance, and without petulance, too deep, too all-embracing to be noisy.

I afterwards knew that she had been at the point of death, that the hemorrhage which so often accompanies the first child-birth had nearly carried her into the unknown. She realized it at the time, felt herself going, going, but there was no alarm or uneasiness. It was like fading away into her elements, passing into something almost as much herself as what she knew, into something familiar, friendly; going out, but not going out into the cold; perhaps into the cool, the moist, the colorful, pleasing half-light, half-life, which lacks nervousness and pain—the elementary, the elemental, the Cosmic, lacking the meaningless stridency of civilization, possessing the long, quiet line of primitiveness! She was so civilized that she could easily dispense with civilization, so sophisticated that she could quietly welcome the approach of the uttermost simple, the dissolving into the elements of existence!

How I loved her, how I admired her! Beyond everything else how I *liked* her! She pleased my taste so utterly. She thrilled me with excited pleasure even at the moment when I feared for her life! As I heard the sharp cry of the new-born, like a clear figure in the foreground against the deep meaning of the mother's impersonal silence, and rushing into the room, saw the strange struggling baby brandished aloft by the doctor, and the pale face of the woman in the bed, the danger of it all, the beauty of it all, almost overpowered me.

And then for days and days I rushed about, doing meaningless but necessary things; prodding the strangely stupid nurse, fiercely demanding of her punctuality and carefulness; alert, restless, awake, watchful, untiring, but always with a deep impatience, always feeling myself inessential, trivial, doing these necessary errands, but withheld from her, not able to commune with her, not able to be a part of her; having no longer any relation with her, a mere spectator of her importance, not an integral part of it!

I wonder if I have not been a mere spectator all my life!—a super-heated observer? Have I ever been a part of her real life? Is not my recurrent feeling of almost intolerable loneliness an index, a sign of her remoteness? In her arms only have I been able to feel united with something not myself, bigger than myself, a part of something not myself, my larger self. Under the illusion of the senses and the amorous fancy I have felt a real bond. Was it, after all, merely an illusion? Who knows? Perhaps it was a real union, a real oneness, but with difficulty maintained, impossible to maintain; continuously, inevitably falling apart, slipping back again into tragic, hopeless separateness.

CHAPTER V

I have written something of the art of love and of its difficulty. One aspect of love, what is called the sensual side, is much neglected by almost all men, especially men of our race and civilization. To exploit the possibilities of a physical relation is supposed to be indelicate or indecent. Reticence and unwillingness is confounded with chastity and purity. Our early sex relations are as a rule hasty and unloving, with no subtlety or sensuousness, merely violent, nervous and egotistic. Sexual life seems therefore to most inexperienced women, even when they live with a man they love, incomprehensible and unpleasant. They often pass years without the specific reaction, the complete relaxation and sensuous-spiritual satisfaction without which the sexual embrace has little æsthetic meaning.

So that women often live with a man for many years and have several children and yet know little or nothing of the physical side of love. And if the physical could be separated from the material and the spiritual this would be of little importance. But words represent merely abstractions from experience, which is a complex flux of all things, held in solution. To the sensitively developed human being a merely sensual relation is impossible; it is inextricably connected with emotion, thought and imagination, with what we call the spiritual. And neither relation is possible to the full unless the other is at the full, too.

A beautiful love relation therefore is impossible without a delicate sexual adjustment. It is the basis, the superstructure upon which fine architectural forms are reared. And it is not an easy thing for a civilized man and woman to have an adequate sensual relation. Each human being is a peculiar, irreproducible instrument, different from all other instruments, capable of giving out music of an original quality but needing the right touch, the right player, who understands the particular instrument upon which he is playing. If he plays artistically, beautiful spiritual harmony results, beautiful relations, beautiful children, and a beautiful attitude to Nature and Society.

Art is long, and we do not at once make the best connection with our lovers. When I first met her, I was not at all conscious of any sensual desire. My relations with women had been casual, fragmentary and nervous, and I had not learned to associate physical intercourse with spiritual emotion. So that, at first, our relations were lyrical and light on the sensual side, playful and athletic, smiling, and to her a little foolish and unmeaning. They were not brutal, but to her they did not seem to have any particular appeal. She did not feel the sad, colorful need of full self-and-sex expression and in her eyes was not the longing left by long nights of mutual giving-up. It was in large measure because I had not learned to be patient and quiet, to study her needs and to care more for her pleasure and emotion than for my own, not realizing that the two were inextricably dependent, one upon the other.

It is probable that women instinctively know more than men of the art of love on the physical side. They know that without the quietness of the soul it is nothing. The deep quiet woman with whom I lived unconsciously shaped my sex relation with her. She taught me the subtlety of the approach, the constancy and the continuation of it, and she herself continually grew in sensuous knowledge. After the birth of the first child, when she had recovered her health, how her sensuous beauty and her sensuous knowledge seemed almost more than I could bear! How brilliant and sensual her skin, how wonderful her instinctive art, and yet it was not then the full efflorescence, not yet what she was destined to realize, when our relations grew more complex and more distressful, and when she had become aroused by other men; then the whole rich consciousness developed and I was the gainer as well as the sufferer.

The first child deepened her nature, and each successive child added to the content of her consciousness. Although it is getting ahead of my story I cannot refrain from picturing the singular enhancement, sensual and imaginative, that came after the birth of the third child, a little girl born in wonderful Italy. The light and color of her skin seemed to come from some central sun within and to give her the rich, destructive look of a glorious fallen Magdalene, which corresponded to the deeper knowledge within her, of life, of sensuousness and of human character. Her beauty was then to me no pleasure in the charming, lyrical sense. There was no light, buoyant love in it, but a biting, harassing insistency, a serious, necessary yearning which was as inexorable as the sea and deprived me utterly of all hope of peace and of all desire for peace. I fiercely demanded sensual misery and unutterable impossible longing, and contentment seemed triviality, meant only for superficial souls. And when I saw the look of uncontrollable desire in the faces of other men, and her quick and welcoming consciousness of it, I cannot describe the kind of torturing pleasure it gave me, as if I were permitted glimpses into the terrible truth, which perhaps was destined to shatter me.

How different all this was from those April days of the honeymoon! It seemed as if thousands of years had intervened, and that just because we had been in part successful in the art of love, had mutually given and taken and partly destroyed one another and accepted from and given to others, and loved children and art and literature, and taken as fully as we could what came to us from life, just because of all that richness, our relation had become one that meant the constant possibility and at times the actuality of almost unbearable pain!

It seems to me at times that all I really care for is sensuality and ideas, and to me these are never unmixed—there never come to me ideas without sensuality, nor sensuality without ideas. My mind seems to have the warmth of my senses and to my senses are lent a hue of meaning given by the constructing intelligence. It was this mixed field on which she and I really met. Emotionally we were often far apart, but always was this keen interest together in the coloring of thought and the meaning of the sensual. So that we have been close together without sentimentality and without what is called romance.

And our relation has thus had at least one of the results that is highly desirable. It has helped us to express ourselves impersonally, has helped our writing, our understanding, our culture and our human connections, our appreciation of children and of Nature. It has done more. It has helped us to an understanding of the struggle of mankind, and has given us social sympathy. Indeed it is frequently true of thoughtful human beings capable of the rounded experience that is called culture, that as the youthful passions—which are the slighter passions—subside, as our cruder interest in women, in boon-companionship, in verses and in art-for-art's sake, falls away or dies, we turn to the deeper personal relation, to social morality, to God. Men of forty who when younger sought women and gold and distinction now try to dig deeper into one relation, fight with insistency for an abstract idea, for a social panacea, or for a religion.

It was not a mere coincidence that after the coming of the first child, my relations to other things than her, to my friends, and to my work began to undergo if not a change, at least a deepening. I saw much more in my chance café companions, in the peddler or the poet of the Ghetto, in the pickpocket and in the submerged generally than ever before. My interest in my work, which was formerly light and suggestive, a kind of playfulness, became more serious. The psychology of the thief and of the revolutionary immigrant formerly amused me as something exotic and unfamiliar. The boon companions and the girls excited my senses and satisfied my love of pleasure. But now all these things came to mean more to me, to connect themselves with my real life. My intimacy with her, the fact that I was having an ever-deepening relationship with her, made it impossible for me to approach anything else with free lightness, with superficial playfulness. Once for all, the deeper harmonies were touched and they permeated more and more all my interests and undertakings. As serious intimacy ever developed between her and me, it developed between me and everything else. I saw something in work more significant than art. Writing became for me a human occupation, not a matter of art, nor of business. A thief was a human being, not a thief; a drunkard became a fine soul in distress, not a drunkard. An abandoned woman became a figure about whom to construct a better society, not a prostitute.

My love for my wife, deepened, satisfied and exasperated with experience, enabled me to approach crime in a passionate and a profoundly æsthetic way. It led me step by step into what is called radicalism, into an infidelity to the conventions of my class. To have one purely passionate relation extends the impulse to be pure, that is passionate, in all things. The one love leads one to the love of all, and the love of all re-acts on the love of one, heightening and intensifying it. I saw everything in terms of the intimate seriousness my relation with her had developed in my soul.

Our first trip to Italy when the boy was a year and a half old was a strange and lovely blending of what had been with what was to be. The honeymoon quality was still there, but it was more sensuous and more significant, and for the time being it was not troubled. It was in the charming hill country where the climate is semi-tropical and everything invites to relaxation. The many hills are capped with beautiful old towns deserted largely of their inhabitants and as pure in form and color as shells on the beach. It represents a lovely death, and over these hills and through these valleys we loved to walk. More often I went alone, but alone only after being with her, in her arms always except on the walks. The embrace was as constant as before our marriage and far deeper and more voluptuous. It seemed to me in that lovely, languishing, liquid place there were only two realities, her embrace and the hills with their swoon-inducing atmospheric mantle.

My feeling for those hills and that relaxing, impregnated air, was indistinguishable from my feeling for her. It seems to me that it was the result of it, that it could not have been without it. Without the satisfaction and relaxation after the embrace, I could not have had that glorious passiveness, that sensuous receptivity in which Nature came to me as nothing foreign, but as part of my blood and bone, as a feeling from within. Already my intimacy with her was giving to external nature a new quality never felt by me before. How I returned to her from these walks and how I went to these walks from her! How she sent me forth and how they brought me back! O, the deep, relaxing sensuousness of it! The long, languid afternoons, the quiet warm nights! And in and out of it all was the little boy breaking in on our luxuries with his clear charm, interrupting and diverting his parents who were caught in a continuous moment of almost impersonal amorousness, so connected did it seem with the old town, the sky and the semi-tropical atmosphere!

As I write these memories of a lover I realize that the woman is hardly more than a shadow to the reader. Or rather, perhaps, she is what each reader makes her; each lover—and this book means nothing except to the lover—will see in her the particular woman about whom he has built his spiritual life—the woman who has realized for him the great adventure. I know if I can tell the inner truth to me it will be the inner truth to every lover. To him the doubt, the pleasure; to him the hope, the disillusion, the pain and joy, as to me—the certainty of her love for him, the certainty of her indifference. To him, as to me, the beloved seems one thing at one moment, another at the next, but always wonderful, always incomprehensible, and beyond all else perhaps, strange—foreign, giving glimpses always of magic casements opening on "faery seas," sometimes forlorn or terrible, sometimes warming and infinitely consoling.

The inevitable is the deepest mystery; and the naturalness of her second pregnancy beginning in these languorous Italian hills did not take from its wonder; rather the contrary. This time to her the new life was from the first a welcome thing. Perhaps by now her nature had become adjusted to this intrusion, so that it was no longer intrusion but completion. Then, too, the first born had become a thing beloved and the little fellow had been rather lonely and bored in this to him unexciting quiet, and she foresaw for him a play-fellow. So this second pregnancy fitted in harmoniously with what she felt in the warm surroundings and what she hoped for in the colorful future.

But these no doubt are superficial explanations. Who can tell or know why she breathed in, so to speak, this second pregnancy as she breathed in the caressing air of this semi-tropical place? Perhaps she had become a more unconscious part of Nature which does not question why the seed bursts and grows in the rich, moist earth. And her skin, giving light and warmth, and suggesting the rich material within from which life springs was like the sun-bathed fields telling of the damp pregnancies underneath!

But a terrible disturbance again awaited this quietly brooding soul. Into her expectant state our daily interests wove themselves with tranquil ease; our literary work, and talks, our pleasant times with friends and all the little things and momentary values which relieve and put in bold relief the vital things of life. This deep disturbance was not this time due to me. I threw no cone at her in her second period of travail; nor did I irritate her sensibility. She did not weep because of me.

There came a bolt from the void—a cable-gram from America telling of the sudden violent death of her beloved father. I remember I brought her the message, fearing for her and for the unborn child, for I knew what that romantic man meant to her. But she took it in the quiet, deep way with which she takes all serious things. She said no word, she did not weep, but it went through her whole being and as we both now think affected deeply the temperament and character and life of the child that was to be. I have always felt that it was a deeper blow to her than if she had expressed it more violently. She took it—as she takes everything—did not throw it off by successive paroxysms, but wove it into her complete existence, thereby coloring herself and the child, introducing somber elements into what her nature insisted should always be harmonious.

CHAPTER VI

WE left the sensuous charm of Italy and went back to nervous New York and its detailed and relatively meaningless activities, and I again attempted, as I have attempted periodically all through my life, to become a part of the machinery of practical existence. But the big deceptive generalizations of philosophy, which I needed in my youth, as I have explained, to attain equilibrium, and my subsequent absorption in the deep pathos of love, stood always in my way when I honestly tried to be interested in what the world calls practical and necessary. But to all things I invariably tended to apply the measure of eternity, and eternity spoke to me through the impulses of philosophy and of love. So that the spur of practical need, which was keen and constant enough to have chained most men to the wheel of necessary routine, acted on me mainly as an irritant, leading me into situations, positions, jobs as they are lugubriously called, but never strong enough to hold me there. I was continually thrown off onto the bosom of the Eternal, where only I found significant excitement and troubled peace.

When our second boy was born I was exceedingly active in journalism and in other futilities, called important by the best people, and a great deal was happening to me, in the ordinary way. But these important events have left no strong impression on my memory. They are vague and shadowy and have not the quality of value. I know they happened mainly because from time to time I come across some record of them. Otherwise they would have been entirely forgotten; have taken their proper place in general oblivion.

But what I do remember as intensely as though it were happening to me at this moment is the look of the second child as he came with a flash of noise into the world. As the doctor waved him in the air to help him take his first breath in this amazing place, he seemed to me older than anything I had ever seen or imagined. When I first met Her she had seemed older and more beautiful and more terrible than the Sphinx, but he seemed to go back beyond all human expression and to go forward beyond it all, too, and to represent the suffering essence of Life itself! He was neither animal nor human, but the something from which they both come and to which they both go!

What a contrast he was then and has always been to his brother! When the first child came, he was a baby, a human baby, and at each stage, up to his early teens, where he now is, he has been the child, the boy, perfectly and typically the happy, playful child, the romantic active boy—so much the boy that as yet there has been little else—he has the boy quality taken to the nth degree!—a beautiful thing, a ridiculous thing, a baffling, incomprehensible thing, a delightful, innocent thing, with open joyful eyes, keen to the color of events, unseeing the unseen harmonies and discords.

To his brother, however, are the unseen harmonies and discords; the child of the sensuous Italian hills, the child who formed its unborn life about the spiritual woe of the mother, the child of sensuousness, the child of disturbance! I have sometimes felt that the blow that struck her in the midst of rich peace and joy must have come from some cold, inhuman artist who saw the tragic form—some smiling sculptor who brutally modeled without regard to human good and evil, thinking only of the line, of the possibilities inherent in the clay of life.

Whatever the cause—and our causes are all of the fancy; we know no other—this second child has been strangely sensitive to all things outside of him. They have filled him with disease and pain, but he has seen their form—their discord and their harmony. He does not live in the romantic world of the pure child. He does not become a Sir Lancelot or a cowboy. He lives in his perceptions of reality, and his instincts to construct. He is always building, building, indefatigably, even in the moment of physical pain and weakness. His mood is changed by the sunlight, by the dampness, and he sensitively understands the emotional situation of those near him; and it is on the basis of the way this wonderful, tragic world affects him that he builds, builds.

I am aware that most people love the joyous and the happy; the robust, the cheerful and the pleasant, the adequate and efficient ones, and these are indeed a part of the strange rhythm of life that holds us all, but to me there has always been a peculiar beauty in those who suffer—not those who merely bear, but those on whom all of life impinges, on whom rush the quality of all things, rendering them painfully conscious and sensitive of the beauty and the horror; those who are affected by the hidden meaning of every event and every form and whose structure, whose being, is therefore always in imminent danger, the meaning forced upon them being so constantly great and unrelenting.

So a part of my love for her—my ever deepening and increasing love for her—were these successive pregnancies, these material signs of sensibility to the spirit of life itself; this, her capacity to receive and to be affected by the germinating seeds of existence, to have her being threatened and developed at the same time, to be struck and to expand, and to give birth to little children, through whom existence passes and who respond constructively to it.

Why do we all struggle for that impossible ideal we call consistency? I do not know unless it is because we are unable to attain it, and our strenuous souls desire the unattainable. I loved in her this insistent sensitiveness, loved to see her receive and use whatever came to her, and I feverishly brought all I could to her. I passionately sought for her the widest experience, used my restlessness and my sociability to bring to her all I knew and loved and enjoyed. I wanted for her the fullest life, and yet when she responded to the charm and power of other men, my emotions were not those of unalloyed joy and satisfaction! I wanted that set of impulses, those spurs to life, to come through me alone!

No, not wholly so, for up to a certain painful point her imaginative impulses toward other men gave me a keen though sometimes painful relish. Up to the present stage in the story these impulses of hers had received no tangible expression. I saw them in her eyes, in her thought about other things, in that frequently unbreakable reserve toward me, that coolness, that aloofness that so often froze my soul and filled me with a violent desire to disturb her or to rush off into the slighter excitements of sex and of boon companionship. And when I did so—the actualities of which were few indeed as compared with my vagrant impulses—she knew it, for at that time I concealed nothing from her. It was a pleasure for me to try to disturb her in this way, too; but something I could hardly bear at times to see was how little she seemingly cared for my infidelities. Was it because she cared little for me in that relation, or because she knew how deeply I was bound to her? Or was it because she was still dreaming of the Lover, unrealized, unknown, that these my acts had little meaning for her? Perhaps all these were elements of her feeling, and perhaps I was wrong in attributing to her that indifference, for at a later time I suddenly realized that these acts of mine had meant more to her than I had thought. The simple truth is that I never knew and never shall know what her real feeling was or may be.

At times, indeed, even then, I obscurely felt that her remoteness, her frequent unwillingness was the condition of a greater love for me than I felt for her; it enabled her to see me more impersonally and perhaps to love me more unselfishly, to see me as apart from any necessary instinctive relation to me. From the start, a part of her attitude was that of a mother. The very intensity of my need for her gave me at times to her the appealing charm of a child. And as her children came to her, I became more of a child to her, and, a seeming contradiction, more of a sensual need, for that element is not absent from a mother's love, and one strong feeling does not take from but adds to another.

I know in my cooler moments of sober thought that I could never have loved a woman who was my mistress merely. A strong permanent desire in me is and always has been to hold all things together, to combine steadily in the course of life all the elements of it. Whenever I saw in her an awakening love of a child, a greater going out to Nature, a richer social unfolding, or a developing feeling for things outside of our relation, at such moments there came a great inrushing of love for her, even a greater sensual desire, and a more exalted spiritual regard. And this broader love for her immediately reacted upon all my other interests,—my work, my feeling about society and religion—giving to these greater warmth and passion. Thus the ocean swells to and fro, the tides roll in and out, and there is a strange, vibrating relation between all things, each enhancing the meaning of all else. So that it is impossible for a lover to have a mistress, in the sense of having a woman with whom he has a sensual relation only, for a lover loves all things. Otherwise he is no true lover. And whenever I saw anew the human being in her,—the mother, the artist, the life-critic—I loved the female in her more intensely than ever!

Yes, I loved the female in her more intensely than ever, but it is only the truth to add that I hated it more intensely too! As I re-read what I have written, I am impressed with my desire to tell the essentials, to lay bare the psychological facts of our relation, without sentimentality, nakedly. But I am also again impressed with the impossibility of it. As I read, it seems like fiction, even to me, who can supply much more than I can write down. I know I have not told enough about how I hated the female in her.

I indeed hated her bitterly at times. I was never indifferent, as she was, but my hatred swelled as my love did; it took possession of me, and though only once did I even take hold of her physically in anger, and then slightly, yet a thousand times have I broken loose in utter desire to hurt her to the foundations, to destroy her morally and spiritually.

I hated as I loved her perfect and never-failing egotism, the unconscious completeness with which she remained herself. I saw and loved the integrity of her nature, its unyielding simplicity, but I hated it too. She never spared me. She was as inexorable as even Nietzsche could desire. Whenever she was uncomfortable, the females' claws were immediately in evidence. I could feel them there, even when she spoke no word. And when she did speak it was a relief, although the words might be rasping and impatient. Because it was unnatural for her to express herself in sound, when she did so, the sounds, if those of exasperated discomfort, were peculiarly irritating. And yet I preferred them to her intolerable silence, when that silence subtly breathed an entire abandonment to her outraged need of female comfort. When at peace her silence was balmy and adorable, but when her feline equilibrium was threatened, her silence was worse to me than all the torments of hell. Silence without positive peace is a plague more unbearable than any of the compartments of Dante's Inferno.

No, never in any real sense did she ever spare me. She never yielded to my constant desire for what seemed to her, and perhaps were, the minor moralities of life. They were forced upon her by circumstances, and slowly and painfully she partly adapted herself to them, but never willingly. By nature she hated housekeeping, and the prattle and needs and noise of small children filled her with a wild yearning to go to the woods and to attain the peace of the savage state. If she could have lived in the sea, she would long ago have become a mermaiden, reveling in the salty, undemanding, sea-weedy, salad-like charm of that undifferentiated monster. Just as she withdrew herself at times from my social and amorous demands, to sink into the bowels of her earth, so she had wildly vicious moments when the children, cooks and neighbors—whose social calls she never returned, and for whom she generally had a blighting, cold contempt—appeared to her as scorpions made to torment her. She disliked them as she disliked bed-bugs and mosquitoes which to her were the most annoying of all the lower animals. And for her to dislike anything meant something far deeper than hatred. She seldom attributed to anything sufficient dignity to hate it. But dislike was a sensation she knew to the full. What irritated her comfort or her taste filled her with an inexpressible dislike.

I was by training and perhaps by nature susceptible to the minor claims of what is called civilization. I had a sense of responsibility about expenditures, about waste, and an anxious, foreboding soul that sometimes saved the children from disease and death, but irritated her beyond expression. I nagged and nagged her, and tried to fit her into the world of our meticulous society, and she, like a stubborn mare, kept the bit between her teeth and went her own intolerable way.

I spared her, indeed, as little as she spared me. I dinned nervously into her my demands. I insisted on economy and regularity, an affability towards neighbors and friends. I kept my many engagements with scrupulous care and I expected her, who had no sense of time or punctuality whatever, to keep hers. And when she did not, I fumed and fretted and stormed and acted like a petulant child.

For years and years I struggled to overcome her in these minor matters of moralities, rather than of morality; and there was constant nervous friction between us. It is possible that the friction helped to keep the spark of love alive; perhaps it was there for some obscure, beneficent purpose. It seems to me at times that it was I who did the yielding, gradually, unwillingly. At other times, when I see the deep harmony now in her relation with children and with her outside world, I feel the distance she has gone. In a way, the years have brought about a change in both of us and in our mutual relations and attitudes. In some measure the nagging soul is dead in me, and in her there is a far greater adjustment to children, neighbors and engagements, a greater feeling for what I have called the minor moralities of society. And as I see the outside world and the universe in grayer and grayer hues, her vision is brighter and more cheerful. Her love of life increasingly grows while mine is on the wane. So now we agree unusually in what Matthew Arnold calls the criticism of life. For my love of existence had a long way to ebb, hers a long way to flow!

CHAPTER VII

SPARE one another we never did; each struggled to realize his own individuality, his egotistic need. Neither of us was considerate to the other. Those pale renunciations which hold many couples together in fragile relations neither of us would accept. In spite of the manifold connections of a life of work, children and responsibility shared, the deeper relation between us was founded not on compromise, but on attraction and repulsion, on a kind of interesting warfare. In the midst of the complexities of our common life, each of us has stood fiercely for the individual soul and its personal needs. Sometimes she has conquered and killed me, but I have never really yielded, and children, work and impinging society have at times overcome her and forced her warmly from her well of damp, withdrawing comfort; but never with her soul's consent; never merely to be considerate or thoughtful of others. Our relation has been divinely lacking in sentimentality and in that kind of morality which takes the salt out of life. We both passionately demanded that our union should add to, not take from, abundance. So that whenever we have found an adjustment it has been a real one, based on unconscious necessity and not on the minor efforts of the deliberate will.

I have been more of a mother, more of a housekeeper than the great majority of men. This was due in large measure to my indifference to the usual ambitions of the male, to business, to conventional art and literature and to the standards of society; and to my practical lack and inabilities, as well as to her limitations in domestic and wifely qualities. And she has been more of a father than the great majority of women—she has gone out to the larger world in her thought, her imagination and her work, and has helped to make up for my deficiencies. So that though we never tried to compromise, each has departed in some degree from the conventional sphere and has contributed in the other's fields. Or, more truly, neither of us has felt any limitation of sex, except the fundamental one, and we have worked out our common life as if there were no conventional career for either man or woman. It has been difficult and painful, but it has seemed to us the larger thing to do, the more exciting, the more amusing, procedure.

Amusing! That is the word she has taught me to use in her instinctively Gallic sense. Mentally, emotionally and temperamentally interesting is what she means by amusing, and to insist as we did upon our egotistic personalities as elements in every situation was invariably amusing, no matter how painful it might be. Sometimes the pain seemed almost to break the relation and separate us inevitably, but that which brought us back with a fuller emotion was the impersonal pleasure of contemplation, which to some extent enabled us to see ourselves as if we were others and to be pleased and amused by the spectacle. Art is a significant amusement, and as I have written, there was in each of us, an unconscious attempt to see life as art, impersonally though warmly. That is why we both disliked the sentimental and why we passionately rejected the considerate and the decent attitude toward each other, which was not good enough for our high instinctive resolve.

The deeper disturbance of our mutual life, there from the beginning as undertones, became more definite as time went on, grew into clear motifs in the symphony of our relation. The essential discord was strengthened, making the harmony more difficult but when maintained rendering it deeper; as it does in the operas of Strauss and Debussy.

About six years after the honeymoon we went, with our two children, to the Middle West where we passed an important year. To make clear the threatening new elements which came into our lives I need to refer to my deepening interest in what is called the labor movement of our day. This interest had grown out of my work as a journalist in New York, and had helped to bring out my natural love for what is called the under-dog. It was a love that had no need of a remoter charm. It had no relation to kindness or philanthropy. It had no pity or morality in it. It was a simple love for the unfamiliar, and for those instincts and basic ideas newly germinating which to my imagination seemed to hold out the promise of a more exciting and interesting and therefore a juster and better society. I was deeply tired of historical, platitudinous conventions and moralities in living and in art, and whenever I found the consciously or unconsciously rebellious I was strangely and pleasurably moved. It was for me an enjoyment second only in intensity to my love for the Woman, and, at bottom, these passions were connected. An intense temperamental element in the love for a woman is the exhilaration of a close relation with the primitive, the instinctive, and the ideal at once. He who has never desired a re-valuation of all values, who in his deeper emotions is not a revolutionist, has never fully loved a woman, for in the closest personal relation there lies a challenge and a threat to all that is meaningless or lifeless in organized society.

I have never been able to learn much from books; or from any other record of human experience. Only when I come in contact with men and women do I seem to myself to think. I then feel the strange inner excitement which is analogous to the thrill of the love adventure. What seems a new conception arouses me as does the kiss of the beloved! My life among the rebellious victims of the industrial system gave me some vital ideas which for a time played an unwarrantably important part in my life and have left a definitely sound and permanent effect. And these ideas deeply disturbed my relation with Her, and, as I now think, enriched and stimulated our lives both together and as individuals.

I saw how deep and all-embracing, and really how destructive of our conventions and minor moralities, the philosophy of the proletarian really is; how it strips society to the essential! It destroys the values we put on personal property as it points out with intensity the enslaving function of possessions. A conception of a social order whose morality, law, art and conventions are formed about the economic advantage of a dominant few startles the mind and the imagination and turns the strenuous soul to an analysis of the fundamentals. It puts him in a mood where respectability and all its institutions seem a higher form of injustice and robbery and makes him see the criminal, the outcast and the disinherited with a new and wondering sympathy; not a sympathy which expresses itself in benevolence and effort toward reform, but a mental and imaginative sympathy which sees in revolution the hope of a more vital art and literature, a deeper justice and a richer human existence; a sympathy which is in its character æsthetic—the sympathy of the social artist, not of the mere reformer or of the narrow labor agitator.

For a year I was deeply absorbed in these ideas and feelings, new and disturbing and enriching to me. And I, of course, brought them home to her, as I brought everything home to her. I took to her my feelings and my impressions, unbalanced and hot from their source; and she met the men and women who were the incarnations of these disturbing conceptions.

Ideas of marriage and the love relation in general were affected like everything else by this far-reaching proletarian philosophy. To free love from convention and from the economic incubus seemed a profoundly moral need. The fear that the love of one's mistress was the indirect result of commercial necessity aroused a new variety of jealousy! In some strenuous lovers a strange passion was aroused—to break down all sex conventions in order to purify and strengthen the essential spiritual bond!

I met men and women who, with the energy of poets and idealists, attempted to free themselves from that jealousy which is founded on physical possession. They longed to have so strong a spiritual bond that it would be independent of any material event or any mere physical happening. They tried to rid themselves of all pain due to the physical infidelities of their lovers or mistresses!—believing that love is of the soul, and is pure and intense only when freed from the gross superstitions of the past. And one of the gross superstitions seemed to them the almost instinctive belief that a sexual episode or experience with any other except the beloved is of necessity a moral or spiritual infidelity. They traced this feeling to old theology and to the sense of ownership extended until it includes the body of the loved one!

They highly demanded that the love relation should be free and independent, that it should be one in which proud and individual equals commune and communicate, and give to each other rich gifts, but make no demands and accept no sacrifices, and claim no tangible possession in the personality of the other. Only so could each bring to the other his best, something racy and strange because his own, something so personal that it stimulated the other, though it might waylay, disturb and exasperate. Their voice was that of strenuous and idealistic youth bearing the burden of a general historical disillusionment.

A burden indeed it is! To accept well marked out conceptions of morality and norms of beauty is the easier way. To try to reconstruct the basis on which our feelings express themselves is a task indeed for the gods. And since men and women are not unlimited, these idealists among them fell frequently and bit the dust of humiliation and despair. Old tradition and old instinct proved stronger than they and, filled with commonplace jealousy, a new pain was added to the old—they were not only crudely and madly jealous but they also hated themselves for being so! Theirs was a new, deep pain indeed! They were no longer comforted by the conviction of being wronged, of their honor outraged, of being soldiers, though unhappy, in the cause of morality. They suffered and condemned themselves for suffering. They did not have even the consolation of thinking themselves justified!

These subtly-interrelated ideas connected with the whole field of the philosophy of total reconstruction with which I came in personal contact through association with expressive personalities among the industrial victims of conventionalized society, had a great and for a time an unbalancing influence on me, and, with my customary need for giving all I had, bad and good, I delivered to her my new passionate perceptions, my disturbing ideals and my fragmentary and idealistic hopes of a superior race of men and women—men and women capable of maintaining beautiful and intense relations and at the same time being superior to the time-worn and, as I thought, outworn tests of virtue and fidelity.

To try the impossible is the function of the idealist and of the fool. And I have certainly at times been a fool if not an idealist in my demands on myself and on her. She took these my new and excited feelings as she tended to take everything in her moral environment, to make it a part of her as far as she could harmonize it with what she already possessed, with what had gone before. And so she began to make experiments which had been in part instigated by me, but which, after all, was only the following out of her deeper nature, a nature more unconventional than mine, and less theoretical. She tended more than I to put into thorough practice what she had once mentally accepted. The ease and calmness with which she could take a mental proposition filled me with uneasiness. I felt that if she loved me she would have more in her instincts to overcome.

I encouraged her to have intimate friendships with other men; to be alone with my friends and with hers; but when I saw in her an eager readiness to take advantage of my initiative, the old racial feeling of jealousy would stir within me. When I saw that other men excited her, and that she often preferred their society to mine, deep pain would take possession of me! One day she coolly told me not to come home to luncheon as she wanted that time alone with one of my friends!

That was the occasion of a violent quarrel between us. When I expressed my dislike at being excluded she accused me of hopeless inconsistency.

Inconsistent I was, but not in the way she meant. My inconsistency lay in demanding from her what her nature could not give, even when I knew she could not give it! Perhaps a part of my love for her was this inability of hers to give herself to me, but I always have struggled desperately to secure from her that absolute devotion in passion of which she is incapable—at least to me.

It was not that she lunched alone with another man who was beginning with excitement to see her. It was not that that disturbed me. It was not so crude as that, though she ironically and contemptuously characterized it so. I loved to have her like other men, as I loved to have her like all of life. To taste and to enjoy and to be stimulated to greater thought and understanding and to more comprehensive emotion, I loved to feel that this was for her. It gave me a vicarious excitement, a warm secondary pleasure, and it fed my illusion, an illusion recognized by me as an illusion, of what she might one day be capable of with me.

And to have her know other men intimately, just as I continually wished to know other women intimately, was with me a genuine desire. I saw in this one of the conditions of greater social relations between her and me, of a richer material for conversation and for common life together. Whenever she showed an interest in other men I saw in it what I call the live line; it was to me an exciting sign of imaginative vitality—I saw the life spirit in her!

Yes, but what filled me at the same time with unutterable passionate misery was her tendency at such moments to reject me! That she wanted to see other men alone and intimately squared with my conscious ideals and even with my emotional impulses and with my need of pleasurable excitement. But that this new experience should make the distance between her and me still greater, this was to me the unendurable. For her to tell me she did not want me to be with her and him, when I wanted to be there, this was an intolerable exclusion, and reopened the old periodic wounds.

I dwell upon this seemingly trivial occasion of the luncheon because of its symbolic character. It was typical of much that had happened between us continually. The thing in her which all my instincts as well as all my philosophy and thought rejects is her inability to feel for me at the moment she feels for another! This is the eternal jar, the perception which takes from the harmony of life, from the unity of the universe. As I have written, all through life I have instinctively and consciously struggled to hold all the essential elements of my life together,—not to drop anything out of what has once been seen as beautiful. In this painful effort to maintain our deeper memory, what we call the soul is born.

This demand for an extended harmony is what made the youthful Weininger so bitter towards womankind, in whom he saw an essential limitation of memory, and therefore a limitation of soul. His personal, unhappy fate made him err in making of this truth a merely sexual matter. It is not only the woman but the man, too, whose intensity and concentration is not sufficient to hold enough together on the basis of which the triumphant soul emerges.

I imagine that at the root of every real love is this almost metaphysical passion—this deep emotional insistency on unity. So that when I saw, as I often did in her, transparent forgetfulness, a dry ability to put herself entirely into the interest of the moment, losing the harmonizing fringe of consciousness in which the values of the past are held, it almost seemed to me as if her soul was damned or had never been born, and my whole being wept at the temporary destruction of my Ideal, at the confutation of my philosophy, at the negation of my deepest instinct.

But how often did I try to be as at such times she seemed to me to be! In a kind of metaphysical despair how often did I try to rid myself of underlying memory! to be a rebel to the soul itself, to live in the dry, hard moment, without fringe or atmosphere!—trailing on with me none of the long reaches of the past! And how often has my unconscious demand for unity kept me from realizing my deliberate desire to kill the soul.

In the arms of other women I have attempted to deny the soul. I have longed to live as if I had no essential memory; as if there were no deep instinct in me to build my life of values about a central principle. When I failed—as I always have—I have sometimes wept bitter tears, tears falling because of my inability to break up my own integrity. I have been with women whom I liked and admired, with whom I wanted to have an absolute and refreshing intimacy. I have sometimes felt that my salvation depended on being able to give myself completely to another woman, and I have at times tried desperately to do so, but She always stood between, invisible, silent, representing for me the eternal principle of continuity in emotion, insisting on the Memory-Soul, demanding, without intending to, a monogamy deeper than that based on convention or law.

Demanding this deeper monogamy, not only without intending to, but even without understanding the nature of monogamy when it concerns the spirit. She made the deeper monogamy necessary for me, but she did not understand its nature! How often did she wonder at the character of my love for her! Her large, frank, mysterious eyes glowed with a kind of contemplative examination. I was a curious and interesting phenomenon—sometimes beautiful and attractive to her, sometimes irritating and unpleasant—but always incomprehensible was the nature of my love, perhaps the nature of Love itself!

If she had at any one moment understood this inevitable bondage of my spirit, a bondage which was independent of any of the conventional expressions of fidelity, a bondage bound up with my feeling about myself and all of life, she would have understood the reason for my jealousy.

I was jealous because she was not bound in the same deep, independent way! independent of conventions, bound by the essential law of the spirit. It would have been easy for me to endure what is called infidelity had the real, unconscious infidelity not been so transparently present. A warm friendship with another man involving sexual relationship would have met my growing social rebelliousness, and would have been eventually recognized by me as not inconsistent with our relation, had that relation ever been securely established.

To see in her eyes a temperamental forgetfulness of me and a vague imaginative hope of relationship with an impossibly charming uninjured masculine expression of God brought me back with an indescribable pang to my own inherent weaknesses, my lack of nervous integrity and to the impossibility of attaining that spiritual unity in sex which to me my relation to her had always idealistically meant.

I wonder if every lover does not clearly understand me! Am I not here writing the autobiography of every man as concerns his love relation? I think these memoirs are no more true of me than of any one who has felt the full possibility of a human relation with a being of the opposite sex.

CHAPTER VIII

OUR second child, the child of her greatest pain, the child bound up with the sensuous Italian hills, was seriously ill at this period. Almost every moment since that time he has been struggling between the dissolution of his being and its regeneration. The full beauty of Her would never have been fully revealed had it not been for the full pain of this sensitive child! He with his precarious and tremulous marvelousness was a product of her unconscious richness. I have now fully known the hopeless superficiality of the lover who looks to joy as the distinctive fruit of his relation; and of him who thinks himself nearer his childless mistress than to the mother of his children. Every new link of the beloved with the wider life gives her greater beauty and meaning, and the perception of her interrelation with all of Nature lends to her original appeal a deep structural power that becomes identified with the total love of life.

Things grew constantly more complex for us. Practical difficulties and trying illness, my growing relations with the rebels whose philosophy became a disturbing factor in our union, and its consequent effect on her, these weavings and developments seemed to carry us to a point, an infinity of moral distance from the simple sensuous honeymoon!—giving, however, to that simple sensuousness a new exasperation and intensity. Especially was this true with her. Her temperamental coolness at times quite vanished in the midst of her deep woe and her growing excitement of life. The possibility of an unknown lover and the tragedy of childhood woke her now to an occasional amorous expression in which she gave herself with the last, sad, wonderful giving!

And thus I reaped the painful joy as well as the pleasurable pain of the new stirrings of her nature toward others! And as those stirrings brought more strenuous disturbance between us, so strenuous that they might have burst asunder the relation, the new additions, the children, the practical difficulties, the growing, deepening relations and experiences brought in a counteracting intimacy which prevented the break between us.

If our relation had remained simple it might not have endured. It could not have endured had it not developed, changed, and taken into it the richness of the outside world. It grew to be so manifold, so connected with all else, that the disturbances of egotistic strife were gathered up, controlled and harmonized by the total structure of our existences—as a sound which may be a harsh discord in a simple harmony is a beautiful part of a more complex symphony.

At the most intense point of my absorption in the rebellious victims of the industrial despotism of our day and in their resulting philosophy of life, she and the two children were away for several months, leaving me excitedly living with my new friends. It was the first time we had been separated for more than a day or two, and in my feeling we were not separated then, for I poured out to her in letters the emotional meaning of my life among the social rebels. These letters were full of an exalted excitement, of a vivid hope for an extended fruitful liberty revivifying and regenerating society, and of a direct appeal and challenge to her, demanding a continuance of the Great Adventure, and exhorting her to live freely and to love me all the more!

With me this time of separation was one of mental excitement and imaginative adventure, adventure with ideas, and with men and women. There was no deep relation, physical or otherwise, with any woman, but I touched and experimented and wondered and glimpsed the human and social vistas that were opened to me. And I passed on my impulsive suggestions to her!

And then, just before I went to her and the children again, a letter came telling of how she had met a man who moved her in a strong, primitive way. He had a root-like, sensual charm for her, she wrote; there was a something in him which needed of her and made her need of him; he was lonely and unsocial and graceless, remote and bad, excitingly, refreshingly bad, and me she accused of being good and that was rather stale and dull, and touched with life's too-refined food and not with the stimulating salt of the earth. In him was the stimulating salt of the earth!

Again, more strongly than ever, there came in me the deep reverberations of a nameless jealousy! How weak were my ideas when my fundamental feelings were aroused! Nameless it was, for we have as yet no name for a jealousy which doubts and despises itself, a jealousy mixed with elation and approval of its cause! In the grip of the pang I tried to justify myself. Oh, why need she reject me at every new out-going? Why compare me unfavorably? Again came to me the old deep wound; she had never seen me! never had liked my real self. Again the intolerable pain of seeing that she had never really given herself to me!

She met me at the railroad station. As she came quietly, calmly and cordially towards me, how wonderful, how strong and self-sufficient she seemed! A new life, which perhaps came from the sense of having a new lover, breathed through her, and lent an enhanced vitality; and to have the new without eliminating the old, this was a fructifying hope in her, a hope I should have welcomed, for it was of the bone of my theory and of my new ideal for civilization. I had the grace at any rate to see her as wonderful. A fresh intensity of liking was added to my love, and for weeks I devoted myself to her with a devouring passion that knew no bounds.

It was a passion full of disturbance and moral agony. Her cool ability to compare him with me, the new with the old, as if we stood on an equality in her feeling, this drove me almost insane!

By nature she was beautifully, cruelly frank; and I with an idealistic instinct for self-torture encouraged and fostered this tendency natural to her. It was an unconscious cruelty, due to that seclusion of her spirit which shut her from a quick, alert knowledge of the state of feeling in the other person. I demanded from her on this occasion an entire, detailed account of her relation with the other man, and she, to my indescribable pain, responded with a lucid exactness which had its fascination, too. Indeed, she never was more desirable to me than when she seemed, through some excluding instinct for another, infinitely remote. I might hate her, but she appeared then as a resplendent being.

I saw from what she coolly told me that she was prepared to give him whatever he needed or asked. Just because of her aloofness she was capable of a rich though cool sympathy which saw him as beautiful partly because he needed—a strong being who needed—who seemed to need her. I felt the beauty of her attitude. To be ready always to meet a need is beautiful. Theoretically and even emotionally I subscribed, but why, oh, why, had she through all these long years never met my completer need with an absoluteness which would have calmed and controlled and rendered for me quite harmless her relations with others?

So I felt the beauty and the limitation at once—the beauty of her feeling for him, and the terrible emotional forgetfulness of me! How the temperamental memory dropped out or had never been for the intenser values of our life together! Before my fierce, uncontrolled reproaches she scornfully called attention to my inconsistency—that made me think and desire in one direction and passionately act in the opposite. She cast up to me my physical relations with women and expressed with cool completeness her temporary contempt for me. He seemed so noble in comparison, for the lover in a much more simple relation, always has the advantage in apparent nobility, over the husband.

And I retorted with what I think was not entire hypocrisy. Despairingly and passionately I insisted that she had as yet shown herself incapable of giving to others without taking from the relation with me that my soul demanded. Never, I repeated, had I been able to forget, even for a moment, even in the arms of another woman, my bond with her; even when I desired to forget it, this spiritual love, stronger than death, was unshaken; its strength was even more conscious to me at such times. I was then more aware of it, of its indestructibility, than ever.

But with her it was different, I insisted. Had she ever loved me in that strange, temperamental way, had she ever had that passionate liking for my real self, independent of my qualities, she would have been incapable of spiritual infidelity; no matter what her friendly actions had been, no matter how technically and conventionally unfaithful she had been, in moments of inevitable sexual movements.

Over and over again I vehemently asserted the difference between the conventions of her sex and of mine, conventions that I hated and wished undone and obliterated from society; but which nevertheless existed and which were a painful element in every human relation. I pointed out how difficult it is for a woman to give herself without the deeper infidelity, for she is told by society that unless she loves when she gives herself, she is evil and unworthy, abandoned; and that that terrible and ugly convention is a corrosive reality even to strong-minded, humorous and emancipated women. I had hoped she, the woman I loved, could rise above this crassly physical measure of virtue, but whenever it came to the test I had seen that when she began to be intimate, or to think of intimacy with another man, she tended to forget her spiritual bond with me. Was it because of this damnable social convention, or because she had never felt that bond? Between these alternatives I passionately vacillated, self-torturing, helpless, morally unattractive, undignified, the ugly incarnation of an extreme unsatisfied need!

One day she asked me, as she had asked me before, not to come home that evening until late. She wanted to spend it alone with him. She wanted a relation in which I could be no part, which could not be if I were there, something excluding me! Dumb rage took possession of me, but at the same time I longed to take the strong and independent attitude, the attitude that might win myself for myself, that might win the greater Her for me—the Her for me that I had never had!

So I went away and dined and spent the evening in a gathering of men and women who lightly talked of love and freedom and society. As I looked on these faces and heard not what they said, I wondered if they felt as I felt, if their lives were as mine, and I knew instinctively that they were; I knew that all lovers understand and that this book is a universal book, that all human beings who feel at all must feel as I feel. In my mind and senses, in my conscious self and in the clearness of my definite thoughts, I was with her and him—not with these my talking brothers and sisters whose faces only I saw, for their faces, not their words, mirrored my soul. Did her being remember me? Doubt of her and doubt of myself came with alternating violence and when I went home I was completely exhausted.

I found her proud and silent, instinct with that torturing and amazing recessional remoteness which was of her inner being, of the inner being of all things. She looked at me with quiet, searching questionings, as if she were looking deep into my nature and wondering if there were any consistency there, anything that remained and endured, anything that was necessary, after all that was conventional and accidental and vain and merely respectable had passed. She was deeply serious and it was with a certain quiet anxiety that she met me.

But her quiet passed into silent reproach as I nervously demanded talk from her. She withdrew into that infinity of distance that I knew and hated, and refused to answer my violent demand to tell me all that had happened between her and him. The strong part for me to have taken was dignified trust, an obvious confidence that the best existed between us and was inalienable. But I did not have that trust. That confidence was lacking in me and I was not strong and clever enough to assume it.

So she with clear disappointment was obstinately silent, and this in spite of my growing excitement and violence. And suddenly something happened which had never happened before and never since, although in after years even more acute crises arose; without premeditation I took her by the throat! I did not know I was doing it until I caught myself in the act. Never had the possibility of using physical violence occurred to me. In my consciousness it was incredible—but here it happened without consciousness! The underlying brute in me terrified me, even in the act itself! At that moment I understood murder, and knew that assassination might become inevitable for any one at any moment.

Terror at myself was followed by surprise at the way she took it. She made no resistance, but in a deep quiet whisper she breathed my name. Her eyes grew big and a profound wonder was in that silent sound that seemed to come from all of her. I think the perception that I was capable of absolute unreason appealed in some primitive way to her imagination. Me she had always regarded as a finally civilized creature, analytical, seeking reason and sophistication. The passion which was me she had perhaps never so clearly felt. At any rate I sensed with a kind of shameful pride that she was gazing at me as at an interesting stranger. Not the slightest touch of fear was in her look, but a wonderful quiet excitement dominated her.

Why was it that, in after years, when the waves of passion came on me perhaps even more strongly, I never again resorted to physical violence? It may be the shock to myself when I felt what I was capable of; perhaps it was the contempt that must be ours when we use the uttermost weapon without reserve. To lose all possible control is the final degradation of the soul. And she, too, never again used her final weapon—impenetrable silence to the same terrible degree. Her silence was with her as unreasonable, as much a part of primitive instinct, as was my violence. And she had on that occasion indulged her form of unreasonable violence to the limit. And my violence had been born of hers. I think at that moment a new fear of ourselves was born in each, and that although we did not then know it we were nearer together than ever before.

At that moment we felt the degree of savageness which each could show the other; and the first symbolic response was a wild, fierce embrace, mordant, painful, without limit, sad with passion, born of the new element of recognized mutual strangeness that had been excitingly revealed to us. And in the languid, unnervous reconciliation that followed, the wonderful complete peace, she quietly and fully told me what I had so fiercely needed to know; and I remember how ashamed I was of my relief when I knew that she had been unable to give herself to him, and at the same time of a certain vague disappointment; perhaps because she was still finally untested and doubt of the inalienable bond continued its periodic possession.

CHAPTER IX

THEN there came three years abroad. Economic necessity was removed to a point where we felt we could devote ourselves for a time to contemplative work—I to those psychological studies of temperament which were so fascinating to me, she to the forming of her experience into stories of human life. Dwelling as we both did in our writing on intimate nervous relations undoubtedly helped to make us more fully conscious of our own relation: and what added still farther to this awareness of our bond was my almost constant presence in the family. This had and has always been so with me, with some brief interruptions. Men who go regularly to their office and are only with their wives and children in the evenings and on holidays do not fully taste the domestic reality nor is made the full test of the personal relation. My being with her and the children was irregular but frequent and extended. All day and all night for weeks and weeks and months and months, then in the house all day and away most of the night; writing, she and I at the same time, I taking my share in care of the children, in teaching them, and in the thousand details of the domestic situation. It was a close partnership, full of variation from the usual, interesting, irritating, and replete with meaning and color.

It was soon after the crisis that we sailed; we were both very tired emotionally, but I think she felt as I did the charm of going off into the unknown together. We had left nothing behind us, not even furniture, and we were taking with us all we possessed, contained in three trunks, with no idea of the future except the decision not to live in hotels and pensions, but to keep house wherever we went. This we always did, no matter how short our stay in a place; we insisted on tasting the life as lived around us, and my domestic partnership with her helped us to get settled as well as unsettled very quickly. That we could bear nothing except keeping house had an inevitable meaning, no matter how exasperating those cares were at times to both of us. We were forced to live together in the external conditions of existence, as in the spiritual bond: it was strong, very strong, whatever it was.

On the steamer we were, I remember, unusually quiet. But I felt in her a new freer interest in other things. She, apparently, thought very little of the lover she had left, but because of him she saw the casual stranger in a warmer, more human light. Her feeling of companionship with me seemed stronger because of the recent experience; the element of additional strangeness added to the color of our common life, although I often relapsed into unreasoning pathos and pain. We were on the whole, however, calmly waiting for the future. We were on a broader base than ever, and, resting on our temperamental oars, there was something that whispered to us of exciting, adventurous things to come, for which we were instinctively saving our strength. I saw but not always with pain the fuller appreciation in her glance at other men as they swung freely and picturesquely along the deck. And on my part was unconsciously forming itself the resolution to attain emotional freedom from her by deeper intimacy with other women. Whenever I felt the full pain of my dependency on her, as I did whenever I fully realized her indestructible aloofness from me, I had an access of hope of attaining aloofness for myself through relations with other women—a hope, however, that has never been realized.

Never, however, even for a moment, have I ever felt any diminution of love for her. Indeed, as time went on and our relations grew more complex, more serious, and at times more painful, that love has seemed more profound, more all-embracing, and to be in a way a symbol of my love for beauty, for Nature, for Life itself.

And now, again in Italy, came another period of wonderful pleasure in her. In the beautiful intensity of an Italian spring and summer we realized ourselves to the joyous full, and for a time with no element of interwoven pain. The pleasures of the senses and of the mind, with civilized companions gracefully and indolently living out their unstrenuous lives, dining with them out-of-doors in the long wonderful evenings, and combining the serious languor of passionate Italy with the nervous charm of an epigrammatic Gallic civilization—these pleasures were of a broader, and more intellectualized but not less sensuous honeymoon, rendered all the more poignant by the recent crisis, hinting always of the possibility of volcanic happenings.

Now again began to stir within her the strange unconscious life, and she was pregnant for the third time. At the period of conception we were reveling in a beautiful, full translation into French of the Arabian Nights. Devoted to the sensuous unmoral charm of these gorgeous, colorful tales we lived a life quite out of harmony with Puritanical ideas. The sentimental and the narrowly ethical were far away and this child was started and was born in an atmosphere of mature sensuousness, in a complete acceptance of what is called the Pagan point of view. The tremulous, early lyricism of young love had given place to a rich decided determination to take in full measure the goods the Gods provide!

She was born—this sensitive little girl—on the Arno, on the banks of the stream that runs through Fiorenze, the Flowering City of Tuscany! And her mother this time felt the exhilaration of child-birth, the athletic triumph in the midst of pain, the accomplishment of the impossible with its resultant triumph. And soon afterwards came that full physical beauty, that springing of the blood and of the body, that intense enhancement of color and swelling of contour which gave her the look of a gorgeous Magdalene; more delicate in quality than Rubens or Titian, but suggesting both, richer and more voluptuous than the early Florentine painters, yet having the recessional purity of the Giottesque or Siennese madonna! No virgin could equal her full beauty. No lover could so richly love a maiden were it not for the unconscious purpose of this ultimate fruition!

My feeling for her at that time did not have, perhaps, as much of what is called sentiment as it had before, and was destined to have again; and I imagine it was the same with her. I liked her with an intense and destructive liking because she was life itself, and she had an impersonal relish in existence which included me, the children, the hills, the works of art, the Italian cooking and the witticisms of our æsthetic and self-indulgent friends! Never before had she enjoyed life, never had she trusted and believed in it, so much, never had she been so willing to embrace it!

Yes, she was willing to embrace it! Or, rather, have life embrace her. I saw that in her every attitude. Her feeling about literature and art, about Nature; the love of beauty, always strong and pure in her, was greatly intensified. And there was a subtle sensuousness in her friendly relations with the contemplative men on the hills; a cool freedom from any recognized bond. In her imagination she was as free as air: I could see this in everything; in a glance, in a sensuous movement towards a sunset, the kind of love she showed for a child, as well as her quiet appreciation of the personalities about her. That innate distrust of life which had always been hers, was in large measure displaced by the fully accepted sensuousness of her experience; art, children, the willingness to have lovers, the sense of freedom. The sense of freedom! How vitalizing, how refreshing, how indispensable to the living of every full life!

And this was in part the result of the sex crises we had had together and these were in part due to my interest in the philosophy of the proletariat! What a strange swing it is from the impersonal to the personal and the other way round! How I had fiercely desired this and how I feared it!

And that I feared it with reason was shown by the development of her feeling for me. Her love for me seemed to increase in impersonal warmth; she loved me more as she loved other things more, as she loved life more, and other people more; but at the same time there was even less dependency on me, a greater impersonality in her feeling for me! Partly through other men and partly through my ideas she had achieved an even more complete independence of me! This was beautiful: this is beautiful to me now, and the very beauty of it stimulated my emulation. I wanted to be as she was: I want to be as she is!

Let me not be hypocritical enough to say that that was the only reason which now began to lead to more intimate relations between me and other women than ever before. But it was one of the reasons. I was ever struggling to be free of her in order more fully to enjoy her without that intolerable pain. And certainly my deep and luxurious intimacy with her had enabled me to understand other women better and to approach them with greater sympathy—just as her experience with me had rendered her a more attractive object to other men, more subtly sensitive and understanding, more sensuous, with more of that amorous pity which a finely balanced woman feels so thoroughly that she hardly recognizes its specific character and is not inclined to think herself in love.

And a developed sensuousness in all things leading to a general Paganism gives to friendship between a man and a woman an almost inevitable occasional sexuality. It is the condition of a fuller taste of personality. So at any rate I have always felt it to be, and so as I enjoyed her more and more fully, more and more did my friendship with other women tend towards the possibility, but not the realization, of the more intimate embrace! Never have I been able, as I have written, to achieve emotional independence of her, but my social intimacy with other women grew more and more intense and my relations with them were limited not by my conscious will, but by that mysterious bond which held my spirit and made it impossible for me to give my real self to another. It affected even my physical make-up which in amorous play will not respond to the conscious will but only to the unconscious instinct. And she held that unconscious part of me on which even the instinctive movements of my flesh were dependent—that part of me she held in bond! How mysterious is that inevitable monogamy, and how it shows that the real thing in us all is something spiritual! And how it points to the impertinence of law and conventional morality which insists on a condition already inevitable if of the spirit—and if it is not of the spirit it is nothing.

On the top of one of the most beautiful hills of Italy we lived and played, mentally and temperamentally. A few hours of writing in the morning when we tried with sincerity to express our innermost feelings about existence, I in psychological documents and she in fiction, and then the long, late, cool summer afternoons when the sun changed from the white scorching blaze of noon to the luminous ball throwing long, cool shadows made of color and form over the earth, followed by the fresh, warm night broken pleasantly in the early dawn by the noisy nightingale or the shrill, clear clarion of the cock; removed from the urgent call of economic need, with much unnecessary energy, and in such an environment, why not play? How prevent, or why, the inevitable movements of the human temperament, leading to the song and dance of sex? It was this song and dance that sounded and vibrated rhythmically all about, among these sensuous, disillusioned, self-indulgent ones, and among the spontaneous peasantry on the olive-laden slopes.

I think it was her æsthetic sense, that inevitable response in her to form, that determined for her the character of her social pleasures. There were two men with whom she played in exquisite, amusing ways that had its own subtle intensity, too. There was a passionate, blue flame of a man who loved beauty as Shelley's night loved the morrow, the devotion to something afar from the sphere of our sorrow. She caught and gracefully responded to the aerial nature of his feeling, humorously conscious of his fear of the full emotional or physical caress. And the other was a relaxed sensualist of delicate and civilized character whose French epigrams were the only enticing things about him. Neither of these gentlemen was in deep need of anything except the flitting pleasures of evanescent thought and poetical expression, and she played with them with a smiling and rather slighting sympathy. But the charm was at times great enough to hold her in amusing converse below while the nursing baby above howled in impotent rage because of food delayed. Her need for the amusement of the mind was strong and constant, but I sometimes had sympathy for the child.

And I went off through the wonderful nights to the cafés in Florence to talk to the artists and the women, to taste the Chianti and the Mazarin, and to indulge in that satisfying mixture of work and play—where work is play and play is work, that would be the solution of the labor problem, and is the highest form of an enjoyment that has no sad reaction. But this passion which has followed me always throughout life, to work on my pleasures and to be pleased in my work, periodically ends in an unpremeditated, intenser situation which destroys both work and play.

And in this lovely place I met a lady with whom I played and who played with me. A certain note of frivolity, of the sad Watteau type, however, insists on conveying itself to these pages dealing with this period abroad. The profounder thing in passion is the product of a keen and simple provincialism; where the spiritual lines are long and intense and monotonous. In an old, civilized place, however, full of detailed beauty, passion is broken up into picturesque and amusing half emotions and incipient, laughing ideas which relieve the emotional strain. So I find in writing of our European experience among the completer products of human personality and art that there is an inevitable note of frivolity, even though it has a touch of the sad and the pathetic; it lacks passion and intensity.

We played together, this lady and I, but we were not on an equality, for I was living with my wife—how strange and inadequate it seems to refer to her as my wife!—and to this absorbing relation were added my work and the children, and she, the lady with whom I played, was living alone. In every way, except in the deeper need of the soul, I was satisfied, and she was not in any way, and that formed an unfair situation which always leads to pain and regret. Following the conventional episode of sex which of course ensued, there came an inevitable, emotional demand from her which I could not satisfy, try as I might; for that called on instinctive depths which I could not control and I had the humiliation of disappointing her, of leaving her unsatisfied and resentful, and with reason. To arouse and not satisfy a need is the deepest sin of all, and that any one who has experienced knows and bitterly regrets. What I condemn even more strongly in myself is that more than once, with others, I sinned in like manner, not having learned my lesson, or, having learned it, not having enough self-control and genuine kindness to take advantage of it.

I have no intention of going through the list of my experiences with other women, of those warm friendships and impossible hopes of emotional freedom and of periodic belief that never in her could I find the reciprocal passion which my soul needed; with therefore serious movements towards others. I touch and shall touch only upon such aspects of these experiences as help to explain my love life, such experiences as seem to me typical of the love life of all of us. And I bring up especially the memory of the lady with whom I played at that time, and with whom pain was the result, because of the surprising effect that this affair had on Her, on the woman with whom I had been playing for nine years, the complex, perturbed and difficult game of life.

I had never felt it necessary to hide anything from her; I wanted my relations to her to be of that inner truth which was independent of all external manifestations and of all conventions, and her apparent coolness towards me and the quality of impersonality in her feeling gave me a greater fancied freedom both of act and of openness with her. But when she found that I had had this affair, she staggered slightly, as from a physical blow. I imagine that a part of my instinct in telling her was that desire to disturb her, to make her feel, which is a constant part of my relation to her. I have told how I threw cones at her; but this one was of unexpected seriousness. I felt that something had happened that had never happened before, something that was destined to have portentous consequences; and it created in me a keen sense of my brutality and at the same time a kind of fear, something akin to panic, unfamiliar and disturbing. Never again, I felt, could I be so open with her; for the first time I saw that at some points she, like me, must be spared. Not that my perception had any great influence at that time on my actions, but it did have upon my attitude.

And her gayety was gone. The sensuous lightness and aloof freedom of her life abroad had flown. We were perhaps as close as ever, but it was a sad closeness, with little of the lighter play in it. It was a time of depression with her, and also a time of unconscious preparation for the most serious episode in her life and in mine—an episode that seemed to threaten at one time to put a final term to our relation. She was not aware, I think, of her deep readiness to give to another what I periodically felt she had never given to me; but it was deep indeed in her, this unconscious, perhaps partly conscious readiness to lose her aloofness, to give herself completely away, and the inevitable followed, for that towards which one's whole nature strains, is, in some measure, bound to come.

CHAPTER X

AGAIN I am aware of the selected character of all writing. No literary attempt, no matter how successful, can do other than trace a thread which runs in and out of a vast complex of experience remaining unrecorded. My sincerity can do no more than catch a small though important aspect of the relations between a man and a woman, and in order to make vivid that aspect all else must fade into a gray obscurity or into a nothingness which is far from corresponding to the reality. That is why the most sincere writing automatically takes on the quality of fiction.

With every deepening addition to our relation there has come to me an ever intenser appreciation of her spiritual and physical beauty. This is true even at the moment of great pain, of disappointment and of anger, showing, perhaps, that my bond to her is æsthetic first and last, a bond of pleasure complete though often unendurable to the point of anguish; yet there was always in it a life-giving something. She certainly came to me that existence might be more abundant. In an indescribable, warm way she has always been for me the Woman, with all the complex marvelousness that that means to the Man.

And in the year that followed, beginning with the shock to her from the projectile of my amorous play, her increasingly alienating depth, her steady recession from me, came to me not as something wrong or ugly. There was a something wonderful in it on which I cannot lay my analyzing touch.

And he, the man, who came at what is called the psychological moment, he, too, now appears to me as even then he seemed, a being of exceptional beauty. He was an old friend of mine from college days, always bitter with nervous unbalance and impatient of the world's futilities, not strong enough to help to set them right, but keen to all hypocrisy and false sentiment, full of ambition to achieve which left him no peace and which prevented any quiet accomplishment. I had loved him for his sensibility and his one-time nervous need of me, and now after long years of separation he came to us, abroad, nervously needing rest, broken down from inner strain and outer fruitless work.

And he loved Her, my Her, of course! And I loved him all the more! Perhaps he liked her—that may be a fitter word to call it; but his liking was that intense recognition of her quality which at the highest point is greater than love; he liked her much as I liked her. She pleased our taste so utterly! And I loved to have him so perfectly appreciate her. She is deeper than either of us, he would say, and I knew full well what he meant: I knew he saw how through her quiet breathing personality all of the elements passed, held by her in solution! I saw he felt her quiet unconscious power and I felt nearer to him and no further from her on that account.

But then there came the old deep pain when I felt again the excluding movement of their souls. I felt near to them, but their growing affair steadily alienated them from me! He withdrew from me and I was hurt, and she in equal measure went farther and farther into that unknown land in which I had no home, and I was hurt more deeply still. As they came together, each departed from me, and this caused again in me that mysterious unthinking pang which by the shallow-minded is called jealousy; but not to feel that pang when the best that one knows is threatened is to lack life's impulse. Oh, how may we be broad-minded, tolerant and civilized, and yet keep our feet firmly on the basic reality of our natures?

They came together as if they were spiritually brother and sister; there is much loose talk about "affinities"; it is a vague word which has become a banality, but between these two there was a spontaneous bond which has never been between her and me. They were drawn together by a nameless similarity; she and I were together, I think, mainly because of my insistent love, perhaps because of a mutual strangeness. I can never understand her and she can never understand me. They understood one another at once; and of course I was therefore on the outside, an interested spectator of a relation I did not understand, but longed for.

When we dwell intensely on any human relation we touch upon a fundamental mystery; but there is nothing more real than the mystery of being in love. And although in after years she did not admit it, and I think does not now admit it to herself even, yet I believe that for the only time in her life she felt the strange, temperamental identity of her soul with another. It is no mere accident that that man, long years before I knew her, and all through our friendship, attracted me with peculiar force, just as she attracted me; how ironical and yet how natural that the man for whom I felt the most spontaneous liking should be the one for whom she felt the nameless something she never felt for me!

Well, we all met, as I have written, abroad, and her depression gave way at once to a kind of strong excitement—the excitement of finding an affinity! And I in the first stages of their affair played the part of an encourager, of an abettor and promoter of their friendship. Then, as always, I longed for her the fullest life, rejoiced in all that heightened her feeling and caused a warmer glow in her physical and moral nature; in anything that took her from her cooler depths. And my ideas of freedom strengthened this attitude of mine, and both together made it easy, at first, for them to come as close together as their souls desired. I still hoped that she might have the bond with me that was the ideal of my life as it touched the personal relation, and at the same time follow all the inclinations of her temperament which were not easily aroused nor too many. Is it an impossible hope, the sign of a deep-seated idealistic folly? I confess, that as time passed and deep emotional fatigue has come to me in ever fuller measure, that my hope has waned, not indeed for its realization for others in the remoter future, but for me, here, upon this stretch of time, in this our present social state which so stubbornly declines to accept the light of the higher reason.

We played for a time abroad; but it was not a light and cheerful play. Somber and intense chords were throbbing beneath our frivolous talk together in the cafés of Paris, and in and out of our wine suppers there was simmering a more destructive flame than that of the spirit of the grape. We tried to pass it off in external gayety and sensuous pleasure, but sad intensity lived in all of us. In me the deeper jealousy was threatening to overcome my assumed and superficial civilization. And in him I felt the strong and nervous impulse to make a radical break, to insist on a new deal which would nullify the past and open up for him and her—my Her!—a remote and faery life apart from all the world! And in her there began a self-destructive schism, an unexpressed struggle which meant for her something far more strenuous than any other situation of her life.

He demanded silently, and more and more in words; it was a fiercely expressed demand, and as his demand grew, mine became definitely aroused, and she was drawn and quartered between the two. This is roughly put, but the expression is not as roughly cruel as the reality. Her nature was made for breathing harmony, for abiding, breathing peace, and here in a deep soul, full of unconventional, sincere feeling, was a conflict which threatened, and later almost took, her life.

We and he separated for a period; he stayed in Europe, and, our time abroad being up, we returned to America, and to a Middle Western town in the midst of those monotonous, passionate plains which so intensely affect the sensitive temperament. Here there was nothing of the civilized charm of the old countries, a charm which relieves the devouring central passions, and renders them relatively harmless.

From the beginning, she hated her environment. She bitterly missed the picturesque detail of Europe, and the long, melancholy lines of the Middle Western landscape fanned her smoldering resentment against me and tortured her with the intense new need which he had aroused, and which his eager, passionate letters sustained and stimulated. It was a baleful music in her soul, and the few people she consented to know in this, her new home, were caught up in the fierce simplicity of the plains and harmonized with and strengthened her mood.

It was a mood of concentrated pain. I felt the inner struggle that was testing her harmonizing resources to the uttermost, and yet I could not relieve her. I could not fail to let her feel my deepening need exasperated by the seriousness of her feeling for him. Scene after scene made vivid to her the reality of my egotistic passion and his letters were one intense, white flame. When he came again to be with us she could not fail to feel increasingly the sharpness of these two conflicting needs. He then had come to know that she to him was all, and with a beautiful recklessness which charmed and terrified my soul he desired with no retreating doubt to take her completely into his life. It had ceased to be an affair with him and had become the serious business of his existence.Now indeed was she disturbed, this quiet and brooding woman! The stronger elements of feeling which I had ever hoped for her and to attain which I had thrown so many cones were now indeed a menace to her very being. She was at last disturbed so deeply that the wreck of all was imminent. When I saw in her lingering look at him the same wondering doubt of what her destiny was to be, sharp memory brought to me that look of hers when I returned long years before and felt her wondering whether after all she was destined to live with me!—that look which was the beautiful, symbolic forerunner of the honeymoon now and forever a sensuous, lyrical joy to me! And here again her nature was accepting, she was unconsciously prepared to see with sympathy this other man, prepared to give herself again, this time with the greater, fuller intensity of the intervening years of experience!But this time to give herself meant a destructive inner conflict. As he well said, hers was a nature of sincere depth, incapable of frivolity. She could not leave me spiritually nor could she leave the children; she could not break the interwoven threads of those twelve years of pain and joy together. She could not refuse my demand, nor could she refuse his demand; she was not capable of the easy relation with him that was not inharmonious with my feeling. For that she cared too much for him. Had she taken him lightly, involving the sexual relation, I could by that time have been reconciled, seen it as not meaning the destruction of the bond I wanted. But this she could not do. She knew as I did that her feeling for him was inconsistent with that she had for me. She was aware of excluding me when with him! It was this awareness that shook her to the depths. She did not want it so! It went against her unconscious will. That she could not fill the deeper need of both of us—and neither of us would accept the lesser thing, even if she could give it—this filled her with a disappointment so keen that it racked her to the uttermost. He wanted all and so did I, and this she knew could never be; and yet she longed for both! She wanted the accepted and redolent past, the old bond, but her temperament eagerly desired the new, the beckoning lover!

CHAPTER XI

IT was him she gave up and then she broke. Ever since the far distant day in Europe when they met, the struggle in her soul had stirred and steadily grown until her nervous system could bear no more. She has often said that in part that terrible situation was due to her physical state, but I think it was the other way round, that her physical state was a result of the unsolvable situation.

At any rate we were all aware that she was very ill. Her calm was gone, and she was utterly disturbed to the very marrow. At last she was what I had so often desired and to attain which I had thrown so many cones—taken completely away from the reserved depths which so often had irritated me. Now indeed she talked, but her talk to me was torture. The self-restraint was gone, which had always been hers, and with an almost terrified fascination I listened to her; listened to her for many weeks while I helped to nurse her back to life and calmness.

We went on a trip together through the sad monotonous prairie country, the first time we had been alone for many years, without the children, with no one else. And she talked to me as if to her own soul. Never can I forget the terrible, the utter frankness of it. I had longed so for expression from her—longed all our life together, but when it came, under those circumstances, it was painful indeed. It was so apparent that she was shocked so deeply that she hardly was aware of her frank revelations! She let herself go with an abandonment quite unlike herself, an abandonment so unlike what had become through all those years the strongest demand in me!

I suppose that it was the first time that she talked with no reserve; and she said to me things which she has now forgotten and could never say again. But to me they live and have taught me much about myself, about her and about the relation which meant so much of life to me. In the midst of my utter disappointment I was yet at school. I knew she was very ill, that she was all unraveled and had for the time given up what held her life together. I knew it was critical. I feared the result. What she said gave me constant anguish, but yet it was not all pain. I, the incorrigible, was still at school, still a Pilgrim seeking spiritual progress, seeking knowledge! It was all so strange! That impersonal love of life which has been mine in unusual measure persisted, and insisted on making a spiritual acquisition from my deepest woe.

As we drove through the long-lined, slowly passionate country, as she lay in restless talk, ever growing more chaotic on her bed of spiritual pain, some of the things that I must always remember, I have set down. Extraordinary they are not, for I think they breathe deep in every noble woman's soul, which is a spiritual abode of deep rebellion against man's conventional moralities and laws.

In and out of her fragmentary and ejaculatory talk were vivid pictures of why he had appealed to her so strongly, and why I had failed. I was to her the law. Even in my criticism of existing laws I was still law-abiding. I was ever seeking a human order. Deep in me the traditional conventions of civilization lived. I was social; I was socialized. I felt the slow, painful family structure through the ages. At the thought of harm to these my soul was ever anxious; I was keen to conscious man's historic struggle with life and Nature; keen to his protecting artificialities. Family life and children, household cares and anxious economies, fear of the future and prudence, mixed though it were with temperamental generosity, were to her as a prison house. To her I was the symbol of the larger prison, the threatening finger of harsh law, the negator of her primitive imagination and of the impulse beyond good and evil.

But he was different. In him she felt a genuine unmorality, a fresh, refreshing, salad-like unscrupulousness. He was capable of a relation to her which had no law, which was connected with no principle, with nothing beyond itself. The love I bore her she saw as impersonal in large measure: I loved her because she revealed so much to me of beauty; it was really the beauty I loved, not her, something of which she was an instrument, as all other things in life were instruments to me of the Divine Something. She felt I was religious and moral, and he was neither. He took her as she was: he loved her, that particular woman, and asked no metaphysical questions, did not live in soul-torturing and impossible spiritual strainings. His intensity was for her alone, and he was willing to break all else and give her freedom—freedom from morality, from anxiety, from responsibility, from law—from me! It was the eternal advantage of the lover over the husband.

I was too good, she said to me, in constant moving criticism. She meant I was not free to be an exciting self, a pure and life-giving form. I did not make the last appeal to her imagination, for I was bound, she thought, by all things not myself. I was too good! How I longed to be otherwise, and yet how fully I knew I could not be but what I was—not good, but deeply careful, carrying with me all the Past, holding all together, insisting on the Soul! It was this, this Soul that oppressed and hampered her. She needed to fly off into mere cool existences, into the soulless places of the spirit.

And then again I had loved her too much, or at any rate too actively; had not left to her enough to do in our relation, not enough initiative; this was a thought on which she constantly dwelt. Her deepest passion was to construct; she needed to build, to feel that of her own will she was bringing to the relation. Her personal work, her writing, had been the way in which she felt she was herself. There it was all her own doing; if she could have felt that our relation was her construction, not mine, she would have loved me more! She had a need to go out actively to others as I had gone to her! She did not so much want to be wooed as to woo! This was her mood, expressed with passion. I make no attempt to tell how I suffered at this time. It seems to me my agony went beyond the point of personal suffering and was a quality of external things—that it was a universal pain, deep and full and hopeless. I lost my habitual nervousness and was calm. To see the woman who meant so much to me thus express her deep dissatisfaction and to feel that she was, mainly because of me, almost at death's door,— well, I cannot say what this was to me. Each man kills the thing he loves indeed! How this woman, like a fly, had been caught, her free flight impeded, by my all-embracing, passionate egotism! I felt a pity for her that was perhaps more unendurable than all else. Then there came the hospital, for her life and reason were threatened. For many weeks she lay in danger, feverishly, unconsciously contending with herself, and I, admitted for a short hour each day, sat quietly by her side, hoping, waiting, for returning strength and self-control. Indeed, it seems to me that it was I who nursed her back to life, for I would not have her go! It was I and her strong will, for that she finally wanted to live, in part for me and for the children, there is no doubt. Life returned with flickering, hesitating fear, and in tremulous lines she wrote me a note in which it seemed to me a new love breathed! And then, a little stronger, she wrote a poem, a ballad of intense and simple passion, in which is told how a mermaid, loving her native salty substance and the damp sea-weed and the unmoral, beautiful sea, meets one day upon the shore a human man and loves and marries him and has fine children whom she loves. But the sea beckons, and one day upon the shore she meets a salty merman, her old deep-sea lover, and upon a gust of sensuous desire goes with him into her native region, where alone she is at home. But after unthinking satisfaction in the depths the thought of her acquired civilization, of her husband and her lovely, needing children, comes strong upon her, and she seeks the sorrowing human, who, in despairing passion, tries to drive her hence! Oh, how wonderful, how life-giving is the power of song, of any swelling art! That she could sing, no matter how tragic-wise, showed returning strength, and a strength that bred more strength! Yes, the tide turned and began to flow, and as it swelled, a new hope was born in her—in me!

CHAPTER XII

SHE had gone the limit of her impulse leading her away, as far as the sweetness and beauty of her nature permitted her to go. She had gone down almost to death, and when she emerged, it was like the phœnix from the ashes. A new spirit, one of willful lovingness, breathed in all her being. There was a subtle change in her attitude toward the children. She had always loved them, but now her love was unimpeded. She accepted them at last! The grace of her demeanor toward them, those deep, lingering, questioning looks at them, these were instinct with a beauty which really qualified of heaven!

And I had become one of her children! The unsentimental, inexpressive depth of her sympathy had been touched. I knew she loved me, and I regretted nothing of the past; the wonderful, glorious, painful past which had led us both to greater feeling for things outside, for life itself; gave us both a greater impersonal love, a love that lacked more and more of the exasperation of temperament, possessed more and more of the pure classic line of unegotistic passion!

Yes, I knew she loved me, and it gave me deep, but not untroubled peace. I could not forget that I had not had to the full the other kind of love—that she had never been "in love" with me! That need in me had never been and never could be satisfied! I feel sure in my reflective moments that had she had that temperamental dependent love for me, she would not have constantly appeared to me so beautiful, so wonderful! It was in part her inalienable independence of me that filled me with so passionate a respect, even when I strove to break it down! The inevitable quality of her resistance, her unconscious integrity, is the most beautiful thing that I have ever known! What so often has filled me with violent despair and fierce unspoken reproach was perhaps the most necessary condition of my underlying feeling.

And now she had fully accepted me, but in the way in which she had accepted the children, the household, and her lot in life. But she remained herself! She could give us love, but could not give herself away! Always mysteriously remote from us, no matter how tender! Not needing, though infinitely loving. How often when I have seen her slow, quiet, humorous smile have I thought of the Mona Lisa of Leonardo; of that unnervous strength, of the "depth and not the tumult of the soul."

A few months after her recovery the new strange life of another child began to stir in her—a child about whose being she fitted herself with peculiar perfectness. This fourth infant, another little girl, was conceived, nourished and born with no resisting element in the mother's nature. It was as if time and struggle had now fully prepared her to bring forth. Her Pilgrim's Progress was beautifully shown in the new life, which at birth filled her with an exuberance never hers before; an exhilaration more strongly shown and a delighted appreciation without a flaw. And this little girl, now four years old, has had a life of unrelieved, gay joy, taking happiness and health as her native element and spreading joy to others and especially to her mother as the little rippling waves give gay music to the long receding shore.

And so perfect was her adjustment that even another blow from the hand of Nature, coming a few months before the birth, did not affect the unborn child. The little boy, always so sensitive, who had been born following the sudden death of her father, was again taken ill, and for months and years we feared not death but permanent invalidism. It was an intense, sad experience for both of us, relieved by its happy result, but taking from me a certain element of my native spring. I was very close to the boy all through his illness, lasting several years, and one effect it had was to give me a greater need of impersonal activity than I had ever had before.

Her going down into the Valley of the Shadow and the terrible illness of the child affected me more deeply than anything else in my life. I had, in a way, been nurse to both of them; nearer far to each than any one else had been to them, and to see these two beloved beings struggling for life, to feel in each the last supreme effort of their spiritual structure to exist, this was more than I could bear without relief.

And so when he had pulled through his long travail in which, child as he was, he had struggled like a hero for existence, and she had, for the time at least, become adjusted to her lot, and happy with her latest born, I turned to work and outside life with a greater impersonal activity than I had ever shown before.

Then followed three years when to a greater extent than ever, I lived among my fellow men and devoted myself more to the so-called larger social activities of men and women, to the work of the world; and was therefore automatically withdrawn more from the life of the family. These activities meant more to me for what I had gone through in personal relations; I think I saw their meaning better, and was better able to act and think maturely. More clearly I saw, more deeply I felt the necessary needs of men and women and their relation to the invisible reality we call human society. For the purpose and ultimate destiny of society is an organized condition in which the relations between particular men and women and their children shall be fully and beneficently developed, where the architecture of human relations may tower to its fullest and most lovely height.

Not only did I turn to these impersonal activities for relief, but as a natural and inevitable development. I am not, however, here concerned in picturing my life except in so far as it concerns my central love relation. This is the story of a lover. These activities of mine were modified by the experience of my relation with her, and my relation with her was affected by the nature of my activities, and therefore from time to time in this narrative I have touched, merely touched upon them.

In these goings out to the world, one set of experiences are peculiarly connected with my relation to her; affected it and were affected by it; my relations with other women. And here I come to a most delicate situation to explain, where to be truthful is probably beyond my ability, try as I may. Only those who have shared my experience, at least in some measure, will understand, but as many men and women, as all men and women who have the imagination and ambition for love, have in some measure shared my experience, though perhaps only in vague movements and tendencies, there will be some understanding of my words.

I grew constantly nearer to other women. I was filled with a passionate sympathy for them. I felt their struggle and their social situation as never before, and I understood far better what is called their weaknesses; and I saw with greater intensity their unconventional beauty. I saw that beauty in a woman's nature has nothing to do with what is called chastity. I saw how little sexual resistance women have, and yet how much they are supposed to have! How their real virtues are ignored and false ones substituted!

In these years I met several women with whom I desired the uttermost intimacy. I had for them the utmost respect and my instinct told me that they were ready for me, ready to give me what I had never had. How I longed to be able to give myself over completely! I did give myself as far as my conscious will permitted, but always, no matter how deep my friendship, no matter how intimate I was with my appreciated and appreciative friend, the unconscious instinct, that deep uncontrollable imagination kept me bound to Her as a slave is bound to its master. It was often to me humiliating and disgusting that I could not be free of her, that I could not go as far with others as my social judgment and my civilized will demanded.

I met women who were disappointed as I was disappointed; who needed just what I needed—who needed to feel a deep reciprocity in passion, a mutual giving-up to the Beyond in each other's arms. And I could not, try as I might, meet those longing spirits! I wanted to, both for them and for myself. I succeeded in feeling deeply friendly with them and they with me, but underlying our friendship was an irritated disappointment....

I had an intense longing to satisfy longing. My deepest pleasure was to give pleasure. This filled me with strange excitement. It was not the desire to do good to anybody; it was far more real than that; it responded to an egotistic need of my own temperament. And the pain that almost drove me mad at times was that She had no need for me to satisfy!

Other women had and how at times I strove to satisfy them! How I almost wept when I could not! How I hated and despised myself and yet wondered at the strength of something in me that was not myself, a something that held me bound to Her, in a way I did not want to be bound! How I longed to give myself to those who needed me, but how I could not take myself from Her who had no temperamental need of me! In this there was a deep, impersonal cruelty, the irony of life, the laughing mystery of the universe.

I imagine that experience increases one's need to give oneself,—to work, to others' needs, to the impersonal demand of Life. At any rate in me this has been an ever-growing passion, and as I felt more strongly about the world, about art and literature and Labor and society, I felt more strongly about women, and loved them always more, and this love was in part a measure of their need of me! I deeply wanted them to take of me all they could— more than they were able! If they could have taken more I would have been more deeply satisfied! It is a strange truth that as I grew older and more impersonal in my passion, women drew nearer to me and wanted of me more, but were able to take of me in minor measure only.

And She who had helped me to be capable of the intenser passion stood between me and its satisfaction! With her I could not satisfy my ultimate longing for she had no ultimate longing to meet mine! But because of her I could not fully meet the need of others and thereby satisfy my own!

I cannot dwell upon these few years of work and of social and emotional attempts at foreign intimacy with my women friends. My affairs were a part of my larger going out to the world and also due to what I at last had clearly seen—that although She loved me, she did not need me in the lovers' relation, and so I could not fully exhaust myself in an attempt to satisfy her, and I needed so much to exhaust myself!—to give myself away without reserve! Important and detailed as these, my human relations were, I can here only touch upon them to the degree that they help to show my relation to her—the central relation of my life—for this is the story of a lover, and it is true that I have loved her only—this strange, cool, incomprehensible, wonderful woman, so beautifully aloof from me, yet so loving, and so little in love!

Since we had hurt one another at times so much there had grown up between us a greater reserve. We did not tend to talk so much about others. I was far less of a retriever who brought back rich human stories—when they involved me—to my mistress! But in an impulsive moment I told her of my attempt to meet other women, to satisfy in them a demand that she did not feel, to respond to a feeling in them for me that she did not feel.

And then again, more intensely than ever, she was hurt. What had happened to her abroad was as nothing compared to this. She was filled for months with a deep passionate resentment—something I had never seen in her before. She felt she had given up much when she broke with her lover; she had, she thought, laid aside, once for all, the great illusion, and had done so because of her great love for me and the children. And when she saw I could not give up that illusion, that I was still longing for the intangible reality she could not give me, again there came to her a destructive blow. She had renounced for this!

Once more there were a long series of frank talks from her—those rare and wonderful though terrible revelations of an inexpressive soul! I found that during all these years of our married life she had felt my infidelities, not exactly with pain, but that they had caused her to retire more and more within herself. The slight but lovely bud of her affection had never been able to flower. Her love for me was more and more maternal, the illusion of sex more and more absent; the moment came when it seemed to be quite gone. Of course I said it had never been, and I believe I am right, that she had had only the possibility of it, for me or for another, never realized. And I told her over and over again that now she loved me, maternally or otherwise, more than ever—that her conventional disapproval of my acts and her deeper infidelity of thought and feeling had not withdrawn her from me, but had brought her nearer.

She suffered, I really know not why, because of my relations with other women—they were not the relations she wanted for herself, and yet she suffered. And when I saw more clearly than ever before that there was something in her which by necessity was hurt by this my conduct, there came a strange change in me. I hated to lose any shade of her feeling for me, and I closed up instinctively my social sympathy, and my natural intimate outgoing to other women ceased!

But my sacrifice, like hers, like all sacrifices, was useless—nay, more, was harmful. My attitude of receptive openness, not only to women, but to men and work, to life, was in large measure gone. My friends noticed that I had lost the keen zest for experience which had been so characteristic of me. She herself began to see that I was older in spirit, that I was sinking into the reserve and timidity of old age, and that my creative initiative in work and life was less. And I felt it, too. I made no effort to be different. I simply was different, and I saw that my work and my life were more anæmic, but I could not help it. Somehow her clearly revealed pain and æsthetic disapproval had for the time at least strangely crippled me. And this, of course, was no good to her. I was less amusing, and still to her the word amusing was of all but the greatest moment. She began to regret my virtue and my old age. She saw that one was part of the other, indissolubly connected. She saw that I had done brutal things to others, under her influence, and I think her conscience hurt her, as did mine. But beyond all else she felt that she had invaded my personality and thereby weakened it, and in about a year she withdrew from her position and tacitly gave me to understand that she would be well content to have me go my ways.

During that year she had been consciously willing to have another lover; she had seen beautiful men whom she admired and who admired her, but deeper than her mind was her fundamental disillusionment. She knew that this for her was not to be. I saw that she was on the look-out, and yet I knew that there was nothing deep in her demand, that she was satisfied with life, disillusioned with what is called being in love, but loving more what she had—children, friends, work and me. Yes, me! She loved me more after all this strange and twisted travail! Even when she calmly told me, as she did, that she no longer wanted me in any temperamental way— that the little she had felt was gone—even then I felt a strange certainty of her love for me! For her love for me was of Platonic purity and strength, unmixed with sex or sentimentality, that seemed to me to be of the essence of tenderness.

She seems now to have given up her futile desire to desire others and to have accepted for herself a deep aloof affection and tenderness for me and for all who touch her. This same she wants from me and only accepts but does not desire my metaphysical needs, my sexual straining towards the universe's oblivion. This she neither understands nor likes. This she feels should be put on other things, on work, on thought and impersonal activity, and she is right, but I, although going in that direction, am not ready—yet.

As yet my soul is not satisfied. It is with a deep unwillingness that I feel her temperamental withdrawal—which in a less degree has always been true of her but never so clearly seen by me. That she loves me more, perhaps, in another way, can never meet that fundamental madness that every lover has. I can never be satisfied until I find the Other—and I know I can never find the Other, and never really want to. I know that what I passionately want is a deep illusion, which can never come. It is of Life's essence, which is to us illusory, as it can never be known and does not respond to our

Ideal. It is a passion that leads to death, but when real as mine is, never leads to satisfaction.

Here I am at middle life living with the one woman I want to live with, hopeful for my fine children, interested in a work I have chosen and which was not forced upon me, rich in friends, in good health, and seeing progressively the sad splendid beauty of Nature and Art, hopeful for man's struggle to break his bonds and interested in coöperating with him, and yet, in spite of all, passionately unsatisfied!

Passionately unsatisfied, and yet to me she is more beautiful, more wonderful than ever! This inaccessible woman, approaching middle age, more loving to me and more remote than ever, consciously rejecting me as a lover and accepting me warmly as a child, her complete and impersonal loveliness, is the one perfect experience of my life, the experience that permeates and affects all others, that has subtly intertwined itself in my love for children and nature, for work and for the destiny of my fellow-men. It has been the sap of my life, which has urged the slender stalk into the full-grown tree with its many branches and its decorative voluminous lines.

The sap still urges its undeniable way; my youthful passion still maintains itself but now more than ever it meets only the rich maternal smile, full of knowledge and a kind of tender scorn. As I write these lines—she, for the moment, distant from me by the length of an ocean—I remember the days when with a certain response she played with me with a light grace. Two little incidents come back to me from the multitudinous deluge of the past—one, when, with the laughter of unconventionality, we openly and completely embraced on the bosom of a Swiss glacier encouraged by the full sun of noon! Again, when, in our fancy, she was the wife of another, and we indulged in sweet mutual infidelity after a delicious supper in a French garden on the banks of the Seine! How we talked and smiled, and how we held for the moment aloof the serious madness that was behind my passion! How we enjoyed the decorous and polite knowledge of the host who ushered us to the guilty couch! And how our French epigrams were mixed up with our light and happy caresses! And at that time, she was beginning to see Him, and I had thrown my cone—my play with the lady in Italy! And this added zest, and she threw at me with more than joyous lightness a glass of wine which stained my white immaculate shirt and brought me to her with a quick reproachful embrace!

Yes, these gestures I must remember, in this the day of the waning of our lighter relations! The waning, yes, of our lighter amorousness, indeed the beginning of the day when she pushes me away, but at the same time the beginning of a love for me that passes understanding, that has no material expression, that is full of compassion, of a kind of dignified pity! A love in which the temperament plays no part, but to which all that has been between us—pleasure, pain, difficulties, work and infidelities—give an indescribable solidity and depth. Nothing on earth can separate us. Our relation, indeed, is built on a fortress which nothing but a double death can destroy, and perhaps not even that!

What is the romance of a young couple, previous to their first nuptials, as compared with our full experience? Why do novels, as a rule, end with the first slight lyrical gesture? Why do we inculcate in the imagination of the young and in our moral code a false conception of the nature of virtue? Why do we imply that chastity in woman has anything to do with goodness, or that physical movements necessarily affect a soul relation? I do not know why we have built up historically these colossal lies which give us pain and unnecessary jealousy and despair.

But what is to me the deepest mystery of all—and this a glorious mystery which distils a spiritual fragrance to all of life—is what holds a man and woman together through an entire eternity of experience. She is to me the key of existence that opens up the realm of the Infinite which, though I can never reach, yet sheds upon all things its colorful meaning. It is only the conception of the Eternal which gives interest to every concrete detail. God inheres as a quality in all things. Religion is right when it points the fact that without Him there is nothing.

Milton Keynes UK
Ingram Content Group UK Ltd.
UKHW030838021124
450589UK00006B/680